Theopolis

LITURGY

AND

PSALTER

First Edition

Theopolis Liturgy and Psalter
Copyright 2020 Theopolis Institute, Birmingham, Alabama
First Edition

Theopolis Institute
PO Box 36476
Birmingham, AL 35236
www.theopolisinstitute.com

Published by Theopolis Books
An Imprint of Athanasius Press
715 Cypress Street
West Monroe, LA 71291
www.athanasiuspress.org

ISBN: 978-1-73516-902-6

The publisher gratefully acknowledges permission to reprint texts, tunes and arrangements granted by the publishers, organizations and individuals acknowledged by page number.

Pages 3-5, 7-10, 13-14, 17-18, 25-26, 28-33, 42-43, 44 (Copyright 1958 *Service Book and Hymnal*, admin. Augsburg Fortress, 1517 Media. Used by permission.)

Pages 61-63, 75, 83, 88 (Copyright by Concordia Publishing House. Used by permission.)

Pages 24, 27, 57-60, 64-74, 76-82, 84-87, 89-105 (Copyright by James B. Jordan. Used by permission.)

Every effort has been made to secure current copyright permission information for the psalms, hymns and service music used. If any right has been infringed, the publisher pledges to make the correction in future editions of the *Theopolis Liturgy and Psalter*.

Contents

Contents

Introduction

"Don't judge a book by its cover," they say. In this case, they are entirely correct.

The volume you hold in your hands is entitled the *Theopolis Liturgy and Psalter*, but it is neither a Prayer Book, nor a Liturgy Manual, nor a Psalter. It is instead a hodgepodge of liturgical materials that Theopolis has compiled for use in our courses and Fellows Program over the past seven years. We like to call it our "Hodgepodge Psalter," and we invite you to join us in doing so. You are free to call it by its given name, so long as you whisper the title and shout "First Edition!"

It is not a Prayer Book or Liturgy Manual because it does not include the full range of liturgical services churches need. Students of liturgy will quickly discover that, while the Matins and Vespers services employ some traditional forms, they do not entirely follow the standard patterns. The *Magnificat*, for instance, is typically a Vespers, not a Matins, canticle. The liturgy labeled "Vespers" is really a revisionary synaxis for a Eucharistic liturgy, in which the *Sursum Corda* has been moved to the beginning of the liturgy. Most importantly, this volume contains no full Eucharistic liturgy. We cannot stop churches from using bits and pieces of the liturgies here, but be warned: This volume requires supplementation.

It is not a Psalter because it includes only a small fraction of the Psalms in the canonical Psalter. Like the liturgies, the Psalms collected here require extreme supplementation.

Now that I have suitably deflated your expectations, it is safe to say we are very proud and excited to unleash this *First Edition!* of the *Theopolis Liturgy and Psalter* to the world. Someday, perhaps, we will release a full complement of liturgies alongside a full Psalter. We are very grateful to be taking this first baby step toward that aim.

In its current form, the *Theopolis Liturgy and Psalter* is almost entirely the work of James B. Jordan. He constructed the liturgies, building on the experimental liturgies he compiled every year for Biblical Horizons conferences. Jim intended these to be catholic liturgies, weaving together Lutheran music, Anglican prayers and chants, a Presbyterian *Te Deum*, and Russian-inspired liturgical settings, all in the form of the Western Catholic liturgy. Jim intended the liturgy to be a teaching liturgy. Over the years, regulars at the Biblical Horizons conferences, and now Theopolis students, have learned versions of many great liturgical hymns of the church—the *Venite*, the *Sanctus* and *Kyrie*, the *Te Deum* and *Gloria in Excelsis*, the *Magnificat* and *Benedictus*, the Lord's Prayer, and the *Nunc Dimittis*. We have learned some of the great Collects and Confessions of the Protestant churches. By moving through the liturgy—literally *moving*—Theopolis students have developed the kind of feel for liturgical worship that comes only by bodily practice.

The Psalms are also largely Jim's work, with some welcome revisions from Paul Buckley and John Ahern. The translations are Jim's, and he arranged most of the settings. Many of the settings use tunes from the Genevan Psalter, revised for chanting. The inspiration for chanting Psalms comes from Jim, too. He has pointed out for years that the Psalms we sing should be as close as possible to the text God wrote. We don't sing in Hebrew, but Jim attempted to replicate some of the style and syntax of Hebrew in his translations. As a result, the translations are sometimes awkward (though, in truth, no more awkward than some metrical Psalms). It is an edifying defamiliarization as it forces us to grapple with what God really wants us to sing to Him. Singing God's songs awakens and sharpens our imaginations.

Jim also insists, frequently, that singing the Psalms is crucial to the church's world-transforming mission. Singing is a sacrificial offering of life-breath to God. The Psalter gives us words to bring our griefs, fears, anger, loneliness, outrage, our exultant joy, trust, and triumphant thanks before the Lord. What we sing shapes us. When we sing together, we shape each other so that we all con-spire the Words of God. A Psalm-singing church is a church attuned to God, ready for the holy war of dangerous witness, the holy war of martyrdom. In response to our songs, the Lord breaks the nations with His rod (Psa 2), puts our enemies to flight (Psa 68) and tramples them like dung on the ground (Psa 83), rebukes kings for our sake, and comes to judge the earth with equity (Psa 98). We would be very different people and would live in a very different world if every church would learn all 150 Psalms and sing them regularly.

We moved ahead with this *First Edition!* for practical reasons because it is cheaper than printing new liturgies and Psalters whenever Theopolis holds a course. Still, we hope even in this preliminary, incomplete form, it will be edifying to the people of God. We hope it will help the church to develop a taste for Psalm-chanting and liturgical worship, and we hope, too, that we will someday be able to help satisfy that taste with more than a hodgepodge.

Peter J. Leithart
President, Theopolis Institute
Beth-Elim, Gardendale, Alabama

A Primer on Liturgy
Jeffrey J. Meyers

Rev. Jeffrey Meyers wrote this Primer for his congregation, Providence Reformed Presbyterian Church, Saint Louis, Missouri, and some specifics apply to the practices of that congregation.

"Liturgy" is not a bad word. No church can avoid liturgy. A church's liturgy is just the sum total of the rituals and rites the pastor and people engage in when they are assembled as a church in God's presence. The pastor and people speak, listen, sing, stand, sit, kneel, raise hands, bow heads, close eyes, open eyes, look, grasp, eat, drink, etc. in an ordered sequence that communicates and embodies both God's gracious gifts to us (Word and Sacrament) and our grateful response to Him and service to one another.

So this is the question: Why do we speak and sing with these particular words and in this specific sequence or order? Many churches today have adopted the informal style of American entertainment, with stages, bands, video screens, casually dressed ministers, and very little reflection on the order of the service. Why have we not embraced that "contemporary" form of worship? Why do we follow the more traditional practice of Christian worship?

Worship Basics

Let's begin to answer those questions with some basics about Christian worship.

First, Christian worship must be *biblical*. We should pay careful attention in the Scriptures to the way that God tells us how to approach Him. The Lord has revealed to us specific precepts, general principles, and numerous examples concerning worship. He is the Lord. We don't get to decide how to approach Him. He sets the rules, not us. It is a lot like being invited into a governor's or president's office. There are protocols set by them, and the invitee must be careful to follow them. We don't just casually stroll into the presence of the Lord of the Universe and say, "Here I am, dude." We are careful to learn the proper procedures.

Second, all of our worship is *a response to God's gracious gifts*. Christian worship has a very important dynamic that is often obscured in modern services. The whole service moves in a dance-like, back-and-forth rhythm of gift and response. The Lord gives; we respond. The Lord gifts us with His speech; we answer back. God graciously offers us an opportunity to confess our sin; we respond in humility and repentance. The Lord forgives us; we answer with thanksgiving and praise. God counsels us in the reading of His Word; we listen carefully and learn. Jesus feeds us at His Table with bread and wine; we gratefully eat and drink with Him. The Lord then commissions us and blesses us at the end of the service, and we leave refreshed and ready for the new week. Gift—>response. That's the rhythm of a Christian worship service.

Third, there is a biblically authorized *order of approach* to God. Or we might put it somewhat differently: God draws us into His presence by means of a sequence of actions that ensures peaceful communion with Him. We've already spoken above about the most important and fundamental structure for the liturgy (and for life): God's gracious gifts—>our faithful response. But within that basic order are other steps as well. And they are revealed in God's directives to Israel for how to approach Him at the altar.

An "altar" in the Bible is a communion site, the place where God meets with and communes with man. Altars in the Israelite sacrificial system were symbolic holy mountains (like Mt. Sinai) where the worshipper, symbolized by the animal, ascended into God's presence (the fiery presence on top of the altar). So how are we drawn heavenward to enjoy communion with the Lord? We allow Him to draw us near through the same steps (minus the slaughtered animal, of course):

1. Confession and Cleansing (the slaying of the animal)
2. Consecration and Wise Counsel (preparing the animal to ascend)
3. Offering Our Tribute (the "grain" or "meal" offering)
4. Communion in Bread and Wine (eating the cooked animal)

So to put this in simpler terms, when God calls us together for worship, 1) we are cleansed through confession of our sins, 2) we ascend in order to hear God's wise words of counsel (the Scriptures read aloud), 3) we offer ourselves and the fruit of our labors to Him by giving our tithe, and finally, 4) we sit down with Him to be nourished with the bread (the body of Christ) and experience joy through the wine (the blood of Jesus). The whole ordered process culminates in our relaxing in God's presence to enjoy a meal with Jesus as the local body of Christ.

Fourth, Christian worship ought to be *saturated with the Bible*. Because it's not the pastor's wisdom or clever speech but the Word of God that is powerful to challenge and to comfort us. That is why our entire service, from the Call to Worship to the Commissioning, is packed with Scripture. God calls us to worship by means of His Word, and our prayers are steeped in biblical language. We hear larger portions of the Bible read aloud, sing the Psalms, and more. And if the sermon is lukewarm on any given Sunday, you will nevertheless have been served well by a service saturated with the Word of God.

Fifth, since the Holy Spirit calls us together and fills the congregation, the service will be *musical*. The Holy Spirit is the breath of God, even the music of God. The spoken word is good, but singing is better. When we sing, we glorify and beautify our words with music, as is appropriate for the dialog that takes place in worship between the Bridegroom, Jesus, and his Bride, the Church. God's Word and our response is glorified and beautified with appropriate music and musical instruments.

Sixth, because we want to express our unity as a local body of Christ, the worship service is scripted. This is so that we can all participate together. We don't just listen to the pastor pray. We will all pray out loud together using a common prayer. Not only does this allow us to participate in unison as an assembly, but it also helps mold and shape us as individuals. Through these repetitive sequences, the Spirit trains us how to pray and how to relate to our Lord. There's no reason to fear repetition in the liturgy. You don't ever grow tired of saying similar things to your spouse or your parents or your friends. Ritual words such as, "I love you" and, "Thank you," along with many other recurring phrases in ordinary life, are foundational for maintaining healthy personal relations.

Seventh, though the elements of the service might feel formal and rigid, its parts are completely relatable to our daily lives. Think about what happens when you invite someone over to your house for dinner. There is a welcome at the door before they come in. If there is any conflict between you and your guests, it will be resolved upon their entrance. Then there's a lot of talk—stories and retellings in the living room or den. The visit will normally culminate with everyone gregariously gathered around the table for food and drink. The evening will end with farewells and well-wishes. Though there is obviously more to it in a Christian worship service, these are also the basic elements of the liturgy. Each week we are invited to God's house to commune with Him and fellowship over bread and wine. And just as you feel rejuvenated and encouraged when meeting with friends or neighbors, it is even more refreshing when we fellowship and dine with the Holy Trinity.

Very Brief Answers to Frequently Asked Questions

Why do we sing the Nicene Creed?

The English word "creed" comes from the Latin *credo*, which means, "I believe" or, "I trust" or even, "I place my faith in." We confess the ancient Nicene Creed as our pledge of loyalty to the Triune God. The Creed is a recitation of the gracious acts of God for us, as well as what we hope for from Him in the future.

Why do we sing Psalms?

We sing Psalms because these are the sung prayers that God has given to Israel and the Church. The Psalms give us words to express the full range of human emotions in prayer to God. When we have the words of the Psalms in our minds and hearts, we have divine authorized content and forms of prayer.

Why do we "chant" the Psalms?

When we "chant" the Psalms, we are sticking very close to the inspired text and not changing the words to make lines rhyme and/or to fit predetermined metrical music. The poetic flow of the words in Hebrew is part of the inspired text and communicates more than simply ideas.

Why do we kneel for confession?

We kneel because we worship not just with our mind but with our body. When the Scriptures record encounters with God or the risen Christ, people go down on their faces or knees. Not only does lowering the body express humility and repentance, but it also helps us get into a humble frame of mind to confess our sins.

Why does the service move so quickly, and why are hymns sung with such a quick tempo?

Worship ought to be lively and energetic because we are in the presence of the living God. Some hymns, of course, are better sung a bit more slowly, especially those that involve either confession or contemplation. But most hymns are meant to be sung energetically and with passionate praise.

Why do we sing so many older hymns?

The Holy Spirit has confirmed the use of many of these hymns since the Church has sung them for centuries. Traditional hymns are rich with biblical theology that engages our minds as well as our hearts. Letting the wisdom of older saints guide us in the modern Church expresses our humility and receptivity to the wisdom of Christian tradition as the Spirit has led the Church.

Why does everyone talk to each other while the wine is being distributed at Communion?

When we eat dinner at home around the family table, we talk to each other. Unless you are eating alone, silence at the table means something is wrong. When we eat the Lord's Supper, we are not merely communing as individuals, as if we have our private tubes into heaven. We are eating as a community, as a body, so it is very appropriate to acknowledge the presence of those around you and pass "the peace of Christ" to them.

Why does the pastor wear a white robe?

The pastor wears the uniform of his calling in the service in order to remind everyone that everything he says and does in leading the service is performed in his official capacity as a minister of Jesus Christ. He's not a businessman, so he doesn't wear a suit and tie. He's not a comedian or entertainer, so he doesn't wear casual clothes or jeans and a T-shirt. He's not a judge or an academic, so he doesn't wear a black robe. He's a pastor to the congregation. As has been the traditional practice in most churches for centuries, he wears a white robe with a stole colored according to the appropriate season in the church year. Just as uniforms identify doctors, nurses, judges, policemen, repairmen, even UPS drivers, so also a uniform is appropriate to help identify Christian pastors.

Why do we follow the Church year?

The Apostle Paul tells us that "everything God has created is good, and nothing is to be rejected if it is received with thanksgiving, for it is sanctified by the word of God and prayer" (1 Timothy 4:4). The Church sanctifies time—specifically, the yearly cycles of our life—with the Word of God and prayer. We coordinate God's created, recurring seasonal cycles with Scripture readings and prayer to remember the life of Jesus Christ. It has been only since the French Revolution (AD 1789) that the calendar has been secularized in so many countries. No longer is it keyed primarily to the great redemptive historical events of Christ's life, death, and resurrection. The calendar has been de-Christianized and politicized. We think there's a better way to mark time that transcends nationalism and the veneration of political heroes.

A Glossary of Terms Used in the Service

Covenant. The Scriptures designate God's personal relationship with us as a covenant. A covenant is a formal personal bond, which has an objective shape and configuration, with promises, obligations, rituals, symbols, etc. Marriage is an example of a covenantal relationship. Sunday worship is called a "covenant renewal" because God graciously renews His relationship with us by drawing us near by means of His covenantal Word and sacramental rituals.

Salutation. Another Latin term that refers to the "greeting" at the beginning of the service. The pastor says, "The Lord be with you," and the people respond, "and also with you" or "and with your spirit." This establishes a bond between the people and the minister at the start of the service.

Sanctus. The Latin term for "holy." This is the seraphic song that Isaiah hears in chapter 6, but it is also sung by the angels in heaven in Revelation 5. The song combines the angelic chorus with the petitions of the people at the arrival of Jesus in Jerusalem: "Hosanna in the Highest." Hosanna is the Hebrew petition to "deliver" or "save."

Purification. This is the name of the first "sacrifice" made in the sequence of animal sacrifices given to Israel as the way of drawing near to the Lord. This particular sacrifice highlights the death of the animal (symbolizing the worshiper) and the disposition of blood on the altar (a public display that the death has happened) in order to begin the process of the ascension into the Lord's presence.

Yahweh. Yahweh is the revealed name of God in the Hebrew Scriptures. The English word "God" is a generic term for divinity, a translation of the Hebrew *El* or *Elohim*. The true God revealed His personal name "Yahweh" to His covenant people so they could call on Him by name. The Jews later decided that it was too dangerous to say that name and instead said *Adonai* (Lord) whenever the name *Yahweh* occurred in the Scriptures. Unfortunately, English translations perpetuate that superstition by translating Yahweh as "Lord." But God's *name* is not Lord. Lord is another word for "Master." That's simply one of His titles. Our Lord and God is Yahweh. And Yahweh came to us in the flesh. The name "Jesus" is the English way of saying "Joshua," and that Hebrew name means "Yahweh saves" (*Yah-shua*).

Consecration. From the Latin that means "set apart" or "make holy." After we are purified, we are consecrated by the Word of God. During this part of the service, we hear the Scriptures read and explained and are thereby exposed to the consecrating power of the Word of God. This corresponds to the priestly preparation of the animal for its ascent to the altar.

Sursum Corda. From the Latin "lifted hearts." It is often put just before Communion, but we place it near the beginning after we are forgiven to highlight that God has drawn us up and near to Him at the start of the service. When we say, "We lift up our hearts before the Lord," we are confessing by faith that we have been admitted into the Lord's heavenly court.

Psalm Chants. The word "chant" has a medieval ring to it, but we often chant Psalms in order to stay very close to the actually inspired words of the Psalms, which make up the sung prayer book that God has given to His people.

Nicene Creed. A creed is a spoken or sung confession of faith (*credo* is Latin for, "I believe" or "I trust"). The Nicene Creed was written in AD 381 and has been used in the liturgy of the Church ever since.

Te Deum. The first words of the ancient 4th-century hymn, which we may sing in place of a creed. *Te Deum laudamus* is Latin for "O God, we praise Thee."

Kyrie. Greek for "O Lord." The *Kyrie* is an ancient sung prayer for mercy. This is not a prayer for forgiveness (which has already been extended) but for God to graciously help us praise Him and make our service to Him beneficial not only to ourselves but also to the world.

Lectionary. The way the Church orders her Scripture readings is called "the lectionary" (from the Latin *lectio*, a "reading"). We commonly use the Revised Common Lectionary (RCL) during the seasons of Advent, Christmas, Epiphany, Lent, and Easter. But oftentimes the Scripture readings are tied to the sermon text.

Gloria Patri. Latin for "Glory to the Father." We often sing the *Gloria* after the Scripture readings and our confession of faith as a way of ascribing all glory to the Triune God for the gift of His wise counsel to us from His Word.

Doxology. From the Greek, "words of glory." We praise God from whom all blessings flow immediately before we offer Him our tribute, thereby confessing that everything we have comes from His gracious hand.

Tribute Offering. In the sacrificial sequence, this is the time when a meal offering is placed on top of the prepared animal sacrifice before it ascends to the fiery presence of God on the altar. Once our sins are forgiven and we have heard the Scriptures read and explained, we then offer ourselves to the Lord as we give our tithe and offerings. The Lord accepts the work of our hands and uses our gifts to advance His kingdom.

Tithe. The word "tithe" comes from an Old English word that means "a tenth." The Lord asks us to acknowledge His benevolence toward us by designating ten percent of our increase as His tribute.

Sacrifice of Peace. This is how the last sacrifice in the sequence of animal offerings is designated. The final act of God is to give "peace" to His people as they eat and drink with Him, enjoying meat cooked on the altar. After we are cleansed, consecrated, and offer our tribute, we sit down and enjoy the peace offered to us at the Table of the Lord.

Eucharist. From the Greek for "thanksgiving." The Apostle Paul uses this word to describe the Lord's Supper as a thanksgiving meal in 1 Corinthians 10.

Memorial. The Lord's Supper is a memorial meal, but not primarily because it's given for us to remember. Rather, when we do what our Lord has given us to do, we remind God of His covenant promises to come to our aid. We memorialize God, asking Him to remember the suffering, death, and resurrection of Jesus and be faithful to His promise to be with us.

Nunc Dimittis. The Latin translation for the first words of Simeon's song in Luke 2. We sing this song at the end of the service because we have experienced the glory of the Lord and depart from the service in peace.

Benediction. From the Latin for "good word." At the end of the service, the minister places the blessing of God on the people and sends them out for service under God's protection. The traditional benediction used in the Church is the Aaronic blessing found in Numbers 6:24-26: "The Lord bless you and guard you. . ."

MATINS

Key to Rubrical Symbols

℣   **Versicle:**   Indicates a line that is to be said or sung by the *Minister.*

℞   **Responsory:**   Indicates a line that is to be said or sung by the *Congregation.*

✦ ✦ ✦   **Ellipsis:**   Indicates that a section is continued on the following page.

✠   **Maltese Cross:**   Indicates that the sign of the cross is to be made by the *Minister.*

Lege rubrum, si vis intelligere nigrum.

Notes on Chant Pointing

A vertical line | is used to indicate bars and the reciting tone.

Where there are more words than there are notes within an accented bar, the words are separated by a ✦ bullet to indicate which words are sung with their respective notes.

SMALL CAPS are used for melismatic bars, where a single syllable is to be sung over two or more notes within one bar.

Some words are broken into hyphenated **syl-la-bles** to indicate separate beats within a multi-syllable word. Accented bars are to be sung one word to each note unless the word is divided by a hyphen.

SMALL CAPS followed by baseline bullets after the **BAR** | ✦ ✦ indicate a melismatic syllable that extends into the next bar. The number of bullets indicates the duration of the syllable in the following bar.

A cross (†) indicates the verse is to be sung as a *coda*, using the second part of the chant as indicated in the score.

Refer to Paul Buckley's "Notes on Chanting" on page 52 for more detailed instructions.

¶ All shall **STAND** for the Versicles and Invitatory.

The Versicles and the Invitatory

TALLIS

℣ O Lord, open my lips.

℟ And my mouth shall show forth thy praise.

℣ Make haste, O God, to deliver me. ℟ Make haste to help me, O Lord.

℣ Glory to the Father, and to the Son, and to the Holy Spirit:

℟ As it was in the beginning, is now, and ever shall be, age after age. A - men.

℟ Al - le - lu - ia.

℣ O come, let us worship the Lord.

℟ For He is our Ma - ker.

The Venite

W. SAVAGE

Come, let us sing for | joy to | Yahweh;
  Let us shout to the | Rock of | our sal- | vation;
Let us come before His | face with ♦ thanks- | giving;
  With | **SONGS** | let us | shout to Him.
For a great | Mighty One ♦ is | Yahweh,
  And a great | King a- | bove all | gods.

In His hand are the | depths of ♦ the | earth,
  And the | peaks ♦ of the | mountains are | His.
His is the | sea, ♦ for He | made it,
  And the | dry land ♦ His | **HANDS** | formed.

Come, let us worship and | **BOW** | down;
  Let us | kneel be-fore | Yahweh our | Maker.
For it is | He who ♦ is our | God,
  And we are the | peo-ple | of His | pasture,
  And the | **SHEEP** | of His | hand.

Today His voice you will hear: Do not harden your | hearts as at ♦ Striving | Waters,
  As in the day of | Testing Place | in the | wilderness,
When your | fa-thers | tested Me;
  They tried Me, | though they ♦ had | seen My | work.
For forty years I abhorred that generation, and said:
A people who wander in their | heart are | these,
  And they do | not ac- | knowledge My | ways.
Therefore, I | swore in ♦ Mine | anger:
  Never shall they | en-ter | into My | rest.

Glory | to the | Father
  And to the Son | and ♦ to the | Ho-ly | Spirit;
As it was in the beginning, is | now, and ♦ ever | shall be;
  Age after | **AGE.** | A- | men.

℄ The Congregation shall be **SEATED**, and then shall be sung the Hymn.

The Hymn

℄ All shall **STAND**, and then shall be sung or said one or more Psalms.

The Psalm

℄ The Lesson shall then be read.

The Lesson

℄ After the Lesson shall be sung or said the Response:

℣ O Lord, have mercy upon us.　　℟ Thanks be to God.

℄ Then shall be sung *Te Deum Laudamus* or *Benedictus*.

Te Deum

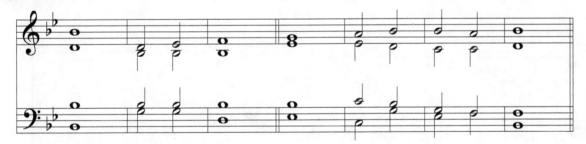

We praise Thee, O God; we acknowledge Thee to | be the | Lord.
　　All the earth doth worship Thee: the Father | ev-er- | **LAST-** | ing.
To Thee all angels cry aloud: the heavens and all the | pow'rs there- | in.
　　To Thee cherubim and seraphim con- | tin-ual- | ly do | cry,
Holy, Holy, Holy, Lord God of | Sab-a- | oth:
　　Heaven and earth are full of the majesty | of Thy | **GLO-** | ry.
The glorious company of the apostles | **PRAISE** | Thee;
　　the goodly fellowship of the | pro-phets | **PRAISE** | Thee:
The noble army of martyrs | **PRAISE** | Thee:
　　the holy Church throughout all the world | doth ac- | knowl-edge | Thee:
The Father, of an infinite majesty; Thine adorable, true and | on-ly | Son;
　　also the Holy | Spirit, the | Com-fort- | er.

✦ ✦ ✦

Thou art the King of | Glory, O | Christ,

    Thou are the everlasting | Son of ◆ the | **FA-** | ther.

When Thou tookest upon Thee to de- | liv-er | man,

    Thou didst humble Thyself to be | born of ◆ a | **VIR-** | gin.

When Thou hadst overcome the | sharpness of | death,

    Thou didst open the Kingdom of Heaven to | all be- | **LIEV-** | ers.

Thou sittest at the right | hand of | God,

    in the glory | of the | **FA-** | ther.

We believe that Thou shalt come to | be our | judge;

    we therefore pray Thee:

    help Thy servants whom Thou hast redeemed | with thy | pre-cious | blood:

Make them to be numbered | with Thy | saints

    in glory | ev-er- | **LAST-** | ing.

O Lord, save Thy people and bless Thine | her-it- | age;

    govern them and lift them | up for- | **EV-** | er.

Day by day we | mag-ni- | fy Thee,

    and we worship Thy Name ever | **AGE** | af-ter | age.

Vouchsafe, O Lord to keep us this day with- | **OUT** | sin.

    O Lord, have mercy upon us, have | mercy up- | **ON** | us.

O Lord, let thy mercy be upon us, as our | trust is | in Thee;

    O Lord, in Thee have I trusted, let me never | be con- | **FOUN-** | ded.

Benedictus

J. Turle

Blessed be the Lord, the | God of | Israel,

For He has visited and accomplished re- | demp-tion | for His | people;

And has raised up a horn of sal- | va-tion | for us,

In the house of | David His | **ser-** | vant;

As He promised through the mouth of His | ho-ly | prophets,

Who have | been since | an-cient | times:

Salvation | from our | enemies,

And from the hand of | all who | **hate** | us;

To show mercy | toward our | fathers,

And to re- | member His | ho-ly | covenant,

The oath He swore to Abra- | ham our | father,

To | grant it | un-to | us,

That we, being delivered from the | hand of ⬦ our | enemies,

Might | serve Him | with-out | fear,

In holiness and righteous- | ness be- | fore Him,

All the | **days** | of our | life.

For the Most High has sent | forth new | prophets,

Who go before the | Lord ⬦ to pre- | pare His | ways;

To give to His people knowledge | of sal- | vation,

Through the for- | give-ness | of their | sins,

Because of the tender mercy | of our | God,

Through which the Sunrise from on | High has | come to | us,

To shine upon those who sit in darkness and in the | shadow of | death,

And to guide our feet | into the | way of | peace.

Glory | to the | Father

And to the Son | and ⬦ to the | Ho-ly | Spirit;

As it was in the beginning, is | now, and ⬦ ever | shall be;

Age after | **age.** | A- | men.

℀ Then shall be sung the Prayers.

The Prayer

℣ Lord, have mercy upon us.

TALLIS

℟ Lord, have mercy up- on us. Christ, have mer - cy up - on us.

Lord, have mer - cy up - on us.

KEDROV

Our Fa - ther, who art in hea - ven, hal-low-ed be Thy Name, Thy King - dom come,

Thy will — be done on earth as it is in hea - ven. Give us this day our dai - ly bread,

✦ ✦ ✦

and for-give us our debts,_____ as we for-give our debt - ors,

and lead us not in-to temp-ta - tion, but de-liv - er us from e - vil.

For Thine is the king-dom, and the pow - er and the glo - ry For - ev - er! A - men.

℣ The Lord be with you. ℟ And with thy spirit.

℣ Let us pray.

ℂ Then shall be said the Collect for the Day.

The Collect for the Day

℟ A - men.

℃ Then shall be said the Collect for Grace.

The Collect for Grace

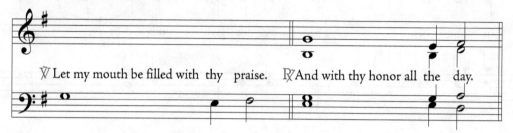

℣ Let my mouth be filled with thy praise. ℟ And with thy honor all the day.

℟ O Lord, our heavenly Father, Almighty and everlasting God, who hast safely brought us to the beginning of this day: Defend us in the same with thy mighty power; and grant that this day we fall into no sin, neither run into any kind of danger; but that all our doings, being ordered by thy governance, may be righteous in thy sight; through Jesus Christ, thy Son, our Lord, who liveth and reigneth with thee and the Holy Spirit, one God, age after age . . .

℟ A - men.

℃ Then shall be sung the *Benedicamus*.

℣ Bless we the Lord. ℟ Thanks be to God.

℃ Then shall the Minister sing the Benediction.

℣ The Grace of our Lord Jesus Christ, and the Love of God, and the Communion of the Holy Spirit, be with you all.

℟ A - men.

SEXT

Key to Rubrical Symbols

℣   **Versicle:**   Indicates a line that is to be said or sung by the *Minister*.

℟   **Responsory:**   Indicates a line that is to be said or sung by the *Congregation*.

✦ ✦ ✦   **Ellipsis:**   Indicates that a section is continued on the following page.

✠   **Maltese Cross:**   Indicates that the sign of the cross is to be made by the *Minister*.

Lege rubrum, si vis intelligere nigrum.

Notes on Chant Pointing

A vertical line | is used to indicate bars and the reciting tone.

Where there are more words than there are notes within an accented bar, the words are separated by a ✦ bullet to indicate which words are sung with their respective notes.

SMALL CAPS are used for melismatic bars, where a single syllable is to be sung over two or more notes within one bar.

Some words are broken into hyphenated **syl-la-bles** to indicate separate beats within a multi-syllable word. Accented bars are to be sung one word to each note unless the word is divided by a hyphen.

SMALL CAPS followed by baseline bullets after the BAR | ✦ ✦ indicate a melismatic syllable that extends into the next bar. The number of bullets indicates the duration of the syllable in the following bar.

A cross (†) indicates the verse is to be sung as a *coda*, using the second part of the chant as indicated in the score.

Refer to Paul Buckley's "Notes on Chanting" on page 52 for more detailed instructions.

℃ All shall **STAND** for the Versicles.

The Versicles

℣ O— Lord, o - pen my lips.

℟ And my mouth shall show— forth— Thy praise.

℣ Make haste, O God, to deliver me. ℟ Make haste to help me, O Lord.

Glo - ry to the Fa - ther, and to the Son, and to the Ho - ly Spi - rit,

as it was in the be - gin - ning, is now and ev - er shall be;

age— af - ter age. A - men.

℀ Then shall be sung or said one or more Psalms.

The Psalm

℀ The Lesson shall then be read.

The Lesson

℀ After the Lesson shall be sung or said the Response:

℣ O Lord, have mercy upon us. ℞ Thanks be to God.

℀ All shall **STAND**, and then shall be sung the Canticle: *Magnificat* or *Worthy is the Lamb*.

℀ A Versicle shall be used with the Canticle.

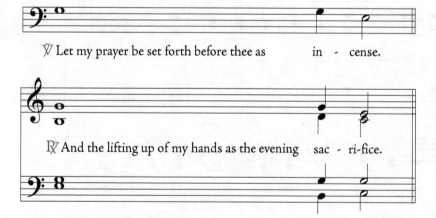

℣ Let my prayer be set forth before thee as in - cense.

℞ And the lifting up of my hands as the evening sac - ri-fice.

Magnificat

S. S. WESLEY

My soul | magni-fies the | Lord
    and my spirit has re- | joiced in | God my | Savior,
For | He has ♦ re- | garded
    the | low es- | tate of ♦ His | handmaiden.

For behold, from | this time | forth
    all gener- | ations shall | call me | bles-sed,
For the Mighty One has done | great things ♦ for | me,
    and | ho-ly | is His | Name.

And His mercy is upon generation after | gen-er- | ation
    Toward | those who | FEAR | Him
He has shown | strength with ♦ His | arm;
    He has scattered the proud in the imagi- | na-tion | of their | hearts.

He has brought down the | mighty ♦ from their | thrones,
    And exalted | those of | low de- | gree.
He has filled the hungry with | GOOD | things,
    And the rich He has | sent a-way | emp-ty- | handed.

He has given help to His | ser-vant | Israel,
    So as to re- | member His | mercy for- | ever;
As He | spoke to ♦ our | fathers,
    To | Abra-ham and | to his | seed.

Glory | to the | Father
    And to the Son | and ♦ to the | Ho-ly | Spirit;
As it was in the beginning, is | now, and ♦ ever | shall be;
    Age after | AGE. | A- | men.

Worthy is the Lamb

J. BARNBY

Worthy is the Lamb | that was | slain
    to receive | power and | riches and | wisdom,
and | strength and | honor,
    and | GLO- | ry and | blessing.

Blessing and honor and glory and dominion be | un-to | Him
    Who | sits up- | on the | throne,
and un- | to the | Lamb
    for | EV- | er and | ever.

Great and marvelous are Your works, Lord | God Al- | mighty.
    Just and true are Your | ways, O | king of ◆ the | nations.
Who shall not fear You, O Lord, and | glorify Your | Name?
    For | You a- | lone are | holy.

Praise our God, all | you His | servants,
    and you who | fear Him, ◆ both | small and | great.
Hallelujah! For the Lord our God om- | nipo-tent | reigns!
    Hallelujah! Halle- | lu-jah | A- | men.

Glory | to the | Father
    And to the Son | and ◆ to the | Ho-ly | Spirit;
As it was in the beginning, is | now, and ◆ ever | shall be;
    Age after | AGE. | A- | men.

ℭ Then shall be sung the Prayers.

The Prayer

ℭ Then shall be sung or said:

℣ The Lord be with you. ℞ And with thy spirit.

℣ Let us pray.

ℭ Then shall be said the Collect for the Day.

The Collect for the Day

℞ A - men.

℃ Then shall be said the Collect for Peace.

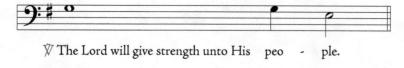

℣ The Lord will give strength unto His peo - ple.

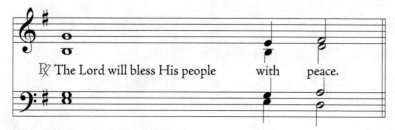

℟ The Lord will bless His people with peace.

The Collect for Peace

℟ O God, from whom all holy desires, all good counsels, and all just works do proceed: Give unto thy servants that peace which the world cannot give; that our hearts may be set to obey Thy commandments, and also that by thee, we, being defended from the fear of our enemies, may pass our time in rest and quietness; through the merits of Jesus Christ our Savior, who liveth and reigneth with Thee and the Holy Spirit, one God, age after age . . .

℟ A - men.

℃ Then shall be sung the *Benedicamus.*

℣ Bless we the Lord. ℟ Thanks be to God.

℃ Then shall the Minister sing the Benediction.

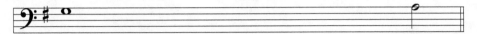

℣ The love of God our Father, the victory of God the Son, all. and the power of God the Holy Spirit be with you

℟ A - men.

VESPERS

Key to Rubrical Symbols

℣   **Versicle:**   Indicates a line that is to be said or sung by the *Minister*.

℟   **Responsory:**   Indicates a line that is to be said or sung by the *Congregation*.

✦ ✦ ✦   **Ellipsis:**   Indicates that a section is continued on the following page.

✠   **Maltese Cross:**   Indicates that the sign of the cross is to be made by the *Minister*.

Lege rubrum, si vis intelligere nigrum.

Notes on Chant Pointing

A vertical line **|** is used to indicate bars and the reciting tone.

Where there are more words than there are notes within the accented bar, the words are separated by a ✦ bullet to indicate which words are sung with their respective notes.

SMALL CAPS are used for melismatic bars, where a single syllable is to be sung over two or more notes within one bar.

Some words are broken into hyphenated **syl-la-bles** to indicate separate beats within a multi-syllable word. Accented bars are to be sung one word to each note unless the word is divided by a hyphen.

SMALL CAPS followed by baseline bullets after the **BAR |** ✦ ✦ indicate a melismatic syllable that extends into the next bar. The number of bullets indicates the duration of the syllable in the following bar.

A cross (†) indicates the verse is to be sung as a *coda*, using the second part of the chant as indicated in the score.

Refer to Paul Buckley's "Notes on Chanting" on page 52 for more detailed instructions.

℄ The Congregation shall **STAND** and then shall be sung the Entrance Hymn.
As the Hymn is sung, the Minister shall process into the sanctuary.

The Entrance Hymn

℣ I rejoiced when they said to me, "Let us go into the house of the Lord!"

℟ **Our feet are standing within your gates, O Jerusalem!**

℣ Our help is in the Name of the Lord.

℟ **Maker of heaven and earth.**

The Collect for Purity

℣ Let us pray.

℟ **Almighty God,**
unto whom all hearts are open, all desires known, and from whom no secrets are
hid, cleanse the thoughts of our hearts by the inspiration of Your Holy Spirit,
that we may perfectly love You, and worthily magnify Your glorious Name,
through Jesus Christ our Lord. Amen.

Confession and Absolution

℣ Dearly beloved brethren, if we say we have no sin, we deceive ourselves and the truth
is not in us, but if we confess our sins, God, who is faithful and just, will forgive our
sins and cleanse us from all unrighteousness. Accordingly, the Scriptures move us
in many places to acknowledge and confess our manifold sins and wickednesses.
Therefore I pray and beseech you, as many as are here present, to accompany me
with a pure heart and humble voice, unto the throne of heavenly grace. Come, let us
worship and bow down.

℟ **And kneel before the Lord our Maker.**

℄ Let all who are able, **KNEEL.**

℟ **O God, our heavenly Father,**
I confess to You that I have grievously sinned against You in thought, word, and
deed; Not only in outward transgressions, But also in secret thoughts and desires
That I am unable fully to understand, But which are all known to You. I am in
need of deliverance from Your enemies and mine infirmities. For this reason I
flee for refuge to Your infinite mercy, Seeking and imploring your forgiveness and
deliverance, Through my Lord, Jesus Christ. Amen.

℣ Arise and hear the good news! Brothers and sisters who have been baptized into
union with Jesus Christ, God Himself promises you the forgiveness of the Father,
the victory of the Son, and the glory and empowerment of the Holy Spirit.
Believe this, and rejoice.

℃ Then shall all sing the Acclamation.

Opening Acclamation

J. B. JORDAN

fff

Hal - le - lu - yah! Praise to God the Fa - ther, Son, and Ho - ly Spi - rit. Glo - ry to You, O Lord, both now and for ev - er. Hal - le - lu - yah!

℃ Then shall the Minister and Congregation say or sing the Preface.

Ascension: The Preface

℣The Lord be with you.
(bowing)

℟And with thy spir - it.
(bowing)

℣ Lift up your hearts.

℟ We lift them up un - to the Lord.

℣ Let us give thanks un - to the Lord our God.

℟ It is meet and right so to do.

✦ ✦ ✦

℣ It is truly meet, right, and sal - u - ta - ry,

that we should at all times, and in all places, give thanks un - to thee.

O Lord, Ho - ly Fa - ther, Al - might - y___ Ev - er - last - ing God:

ℂ Here insert the Proper Preface for the day.

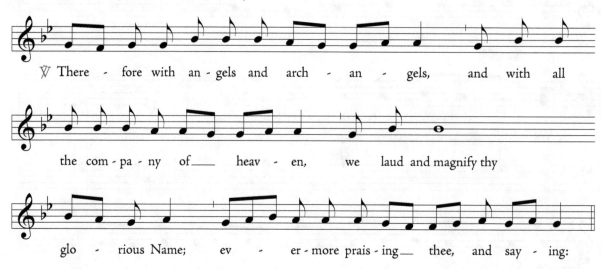

℣ There - fore with an - gels and arch - an - gels, and with all

the com - pa - ny of___ heav - en, we laud and magnify thy

glo - rious Name; ev - er - more prais - ing___ thee, and say - ing:

❡ Then shall all sing the *Sanctus*.

Sanctus

J. B. Jordan

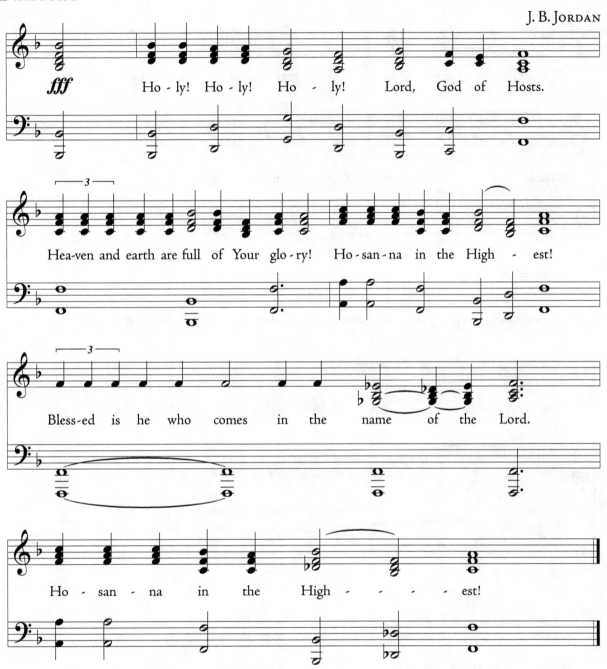

fff

Ho - ly! Ho - ly! Ho - ly! Lord, God of Hosts.

Hea-ven and earth are full of Your glo-ry! Ho-san-na in the High - est!

Bless-ed is he who comes in the name of the Lord.

Ho - san - na in the High - - - est!

℄ Then shall the Minister and Congregation say or sing the *Kyrie*.

Kyrie

℣ In _____ peace let us pray to the Lord.

℟ Lord, - - - have ___ mer - cy.

℣ For the peace that is from a - bove, and for the sal -

va - tion of our souls, let us pray to the Lord.

℟ Lord, - - - have ___ mer - cy.

℣ For the peace of the whole world, for the well - be - ing of the church - es

of God, and for the u - ni - ty of all, let us pray to the Lord.

℟ Lord, - - - have mercy.

℣ For this ho - ly house, and for them that in faith, pi - e - ty and fear

of God of - fer here their wor - ship and praise, let us pray to the Lord.

℟ Lord - - - have mer - cy.

℣ Help, save, pi - ty and de - fend us, O God, by thy grace.

℟ A - men.

℄ Then shall be sung *Gloria in Excelsis*.

Gloria in Excelsis

O＿ Lord, the on-ly be-got-ten Son, Je-sus Christ; O＿ Lord God,

Lamb＿ of God, Son of the Fa - ther, that tak-est a - way the

sin of the world, have mer-cy up-on us, Thou that tak-est a-

way the sin of the world, re-ceive our prayer. Thou that sit-test at the

right hand of God the Fa - ther, have＿ mer - cy up-on＿ us.

For thou on - ly art ho - ly; thou on - ly art the Lord;

thou on - ly, O Christ, with the Ho - ly Ghost, art most

high _____ in the glo - ry of God the ___ Fa - ther. A - men.

℘ Then the Minister shall say:

℣ Let us pray.

℘ Then shall the Minister say the Collect for the Day.

The Collect

℘ The Collect ended, the Congregation shall sing or say:

℞ A - men.

℄ The Congregation shall be **SEATED**, and then the Gradual shall be sung.

Gradual Psalm

℄ After the Gradual, the Minister shall say:

℣ A reading from the Gospel according to _____ .

℄ The Congregation shall **STAND** and sing:

The Gospel Reading

℣ The Gospel of the Kingdom.

℄ The Congregation shall respond by singing:

℄ Then shall all say or sing the Nicene or Athanasian Creed.

The Creed

The Athanasian Creed (Part 1)

The Catholic Faith is this:

That we worship one God in Trinity, and Trinity in Unity,
Neither confounding the Persons, nor dividing the Substance.
For there is one Person of the Father, another of the Son, and another of
    the Holy Spirit.
But the Godhead of the Father, of the Son, and of the Holy Spirit, is all one,
the Glory equal,
the Majesty co-eternal.

Such as the Father is, such is the Son, and such is the Holy Spirit.
The Father uncreated, the Son uncreated; and the Holy Ghost uncreated.
The Father incomprehensible; the Son incomprehensible; and the Holy Spirit
    incomprehensible.
The Father eternal; the Son eternal; and the Holy Spirit eternal.
And yet they are not three eternals; but one eternal.
As also there are not three incomprehensibles, nor three uncreated,
but one uncreated; and one incomprehensible.

So likewise the Father is Almighty; the Son Almighty; and the Holy Spirit Almighty.
And yet they are not three Almighties, but one Almighty.
So the Father is God; the Son is God; and the Holy Spirit is God.
And yet they are not three Gods; but one God.
So likewise the Father is Lord; the Son Lord; and the Holy Spirit Lord.
And yet not three Lords; but one Lord.

For like as we are compelled by the Christian verity to acknowledge every Person by
    himself to be God and Lord,
So are we forbidden by the catholic religion to say there are three Gods, or three Lords.

The Father is made of none; neither created, nor begotten.
The Son is of the Father alone; not made, nor created; but begotten.
The Holy Spirit is of the Father and of the Son;
neither made, nor created, nor begotten; but proceeding.
So there is one Father, not three Fathers;
one Son, not three Sons;
one Holy Spirit, not three Holy Spirits.

And in this Trinity none is afore, or after another;
none is greater, or less than another.
But the whole three Persons are co-eternal together, and co-equal.
So that in all things, as is aforesaid;
the Unity in Trinity, and the Trinity in Unity, is to be worshipped.

Amen.

The Nicene Creed

We be-lieve in one God: The Fa - ther Al-migh-ty,

ma - ker of hea - ven and earth   and of all things vi - si - ble and in - vi - si - ble.

and in one Lord: Je - sus Christ,   the on - ly be - got - ten son of God,   be - got - ten

from His Fa - ther be - fore all the a - ges: God from God;   Light from Light;

True God from True God;   be - got - ten,   not made;

in ful - fill - ment of the Scrip - tures;

and as - cen - ded in - to hea - ven and is seat - ed at the right hand of the Fa - ther,

and shall come a - gain with glo - ry to judge the liv - ing and the dead;

His king - dom shall have no end; and in the Ho - ly Spi - rit: the Lord,

and the gi - ver of life; who pro - ceeds from the Fa - ther and the Son,

✦ ✦ ✦

who with the Fa - ther and the Son to - geth - er is wor - shipped and glo - ri - fied;

who spoke through the pro - phets and in one ho - ly ca - tho - lic and a - pos - to - lic church;

we ac - know - ledge one bap - tism for the re - mis - sion of sins;

and we look for the re - sur - rec - tion of the dead,

and the life of the age to come. A - men.

℃ The Congregation is **SEATED**. Then shall follow the Sermon.

The Sermon

℃ The Sermon being ended, the Minister shall then say:

℣ The peace of God, which passeth all understanding,
keep your hearts and minds through Christ Jesus.

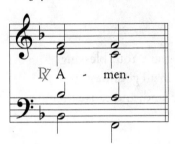

℃ The Congregation shall **STAND**, and then shall be said the Prayer of the Church.

The Prayer of the Church

℣ Let us pray.

Almighty God, Father of our Lord Jesus Christ, we give You praise and thanks for all Your goodness and tender mercies. We bless You for the love that created us, and that sustains us day by day. We praise You for the gift of Your Son, our Savior, through whom You have made known Your will and grace. We thank You for the Holy Spirit, our Comforter; for the holy Church, for the means of grace, for the lives of all faithful and godly people, and for the hope of the life to come. Help us to treasure in our hearts all that our Lord has done for us, and enable us to show our thankfulness by lives that are given wholly to Your service.

Lord, hear our prayer!

℟ **For You are gracious.**

℣ Save and defend Your Church universal, purchased with the precious blood of Jesus Christ. Give to her pastors and ministers endowed with Your Holy Spirit, and strengthen her through the Word and the holy sacraments. Make her perfect in love and in all good works, and establish her in the faith delivered to the saints. Sanctify and unite Your people in all the world, that one holy, catholic, and apostolic Church may bear witness to You, the God and Father of all.

Lord, hear our prayer!

℟ **For You are gracious.**

◆ ◆ ◆

℣ We humbly entreat You for all sorts and conditions of men, that You would be pleased to make Your ways known unto them, Your salvation to all nations. Send forth Your light and Your truth into all the earth. Raise up, we pray, faithful servants to labor in the gospel at home and in distant lands.

Lord, hear our prayer!

℟ **For You are gracious.**

℣ Preserve our nation in righteousness and in true honor, and grant Your blessings to us as a people, that we may lead a quiet and peaceable life in all godliness and honesty. Grant health and favor to all who bear office in our land, and cause them to acknowledge and obey Your holy will.

Lord, hear our prayer!

℟ **For You are gracious.**

℣ God of all comfort and protection, we bring before You all who are in any wise afflicted, all persons oppressed with poverty, sickness, unemployment, or other trouble of body or mind, especially those whom we now name in our hearts before You. . . . Grant them the consolations of which they have need, and overrule their present sufferings to their eternal good. Remember those who suffer persecution for the faith. Have mercy upon those to whom death draws near. Bring consolation to those in sorrow or mourning. And to all grant a measure of Your love, taking them into Your tender care.

Lord, hear our prayer!

℟ **For You are gracious.**

℣ We rejoice with thanksgiving in all those who have loved and served You in Your Church on earth, and who now rest from their labors. Keep us in fellowship with all Your people, and bring us at length to the joy of Your everlasting kingdom.

Lord, hear our prayer!

℟ **For You are gracious.**

℣ All these things, and whatever else You see that we need, grant us, O Father, for the sake of Jesus Christ Your Son, who died and rose again and now lives and reigns with You and Holy Spirit, one God, age after age.

And now as Your Son has taught us, we are bold to pray:

℣ Our Fa - ther, ℟ Who art in heav - en, Hal - low - ed be Thy Name. Thy king - dom come.

Thy will be done, on earth as it is in heav - en. Give us this day our dai - ly bread.

And for - give us our tres - pass - es, as we for - give those who tres - pass a - gainst us.

And lead us not in - to temp - ta - tion, But de - liv - er us from e - vil. For Thine

is the king - dom, and the pow'r and the glo - ry, for - ev - er and ev - er. A - men.

℃ Then shall the Minister say:

℣ The peace of the Lord be with you al - ways.

Nunc Dimittis

℟ Mas - ter, let your ser - vant de - part - in peace, ac - cord - ing to Your Word. For mine eyes have seen Your sal - va - tion, which You have pre - pared - be - fore the face of all peo - ple. A light of re - ve - la - tion for the - Gen - tiles

and the glo - ry of Your peo - ple Is - - - ra - el.

Glo - ry to the Fa - ther, and to the Son, and to the

Ho - ly Spi - rit, as it was in the be - gin - ning, is now and

ev - - er shall be; age - af - ter age. A - men.

ℂ Then shall be said or sung the Benediction.

The Benediction

℣ Kneel and receive God's blessing.

ℭ Those who are able shall **KNEEL** on one knee and face the Minister.

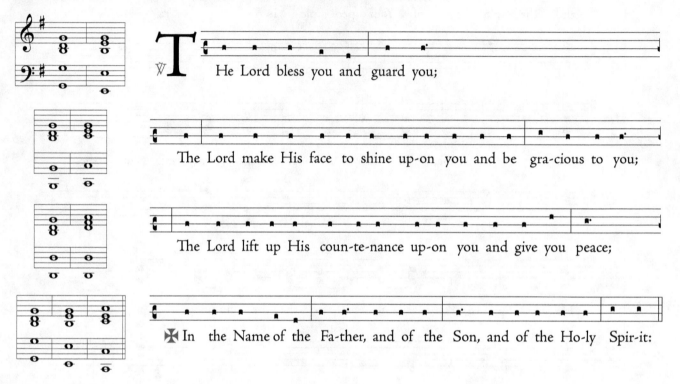

℣ The Lord bless you and guard you;

The Lord make His face to shine up-on you and be gra-cious to you;

The Lord lift up His coun-te-nance up-on you and give you peace;

✠ In the Name of the Fa-ther, and of the Son, and of the Ho-ly Spir-it:

ℭ The Congregation, as they **STAND**, shall sing:

℟ A - men, A - men, A - - - men.

The Closing Hymn

ℭ As the Closing Hymn is sung, the Minister shall recess from the sanctuary.

THE
PSALTER

Introduction to the Psalter
James B. Jordan

The translations presented here are a work in progress. We hope to get feedback from those who use this material. In this Introduction, we set forth how we are doing this and why.

The Structure of the Psalter

To begin with, the structure of the psalter. The book of Psalms as we have it today is not the psalter used at Solomon's Temple, but the completed and reorganized psalter for the Second Temple, the Temple after the exile. This is clear from Psalm 137, which was written at the exile. It is also clear in that psalms by David are found scattered throughout the whole psalter. The psalter used in Solomon's Temple may well have been arranged quite differently, but while that psalter was inspired and authoritative for that time, what we have today is a rearranged and completed psalter, equally inspired and authoritative, as well as final.

We don't know whom God inspired to produce the final psalter. We can guess at Ezra, since he was a priest, and much involved with setting up the Second Temple order right after the return from Babylon.

The psalter now consists of five books, each of which ends with a doxology.

I: 1-41 (41:13)
II: 42-72 (72:18-19)
III: 73-89 (89:52)
IV: 90-106 (106:48)
V: 107-150 (105:6)

It is likely that the doxology for a given book was sung at the end of all the psalms in that book, as the Gloria Patri is sung at the end of psalms in liturgical churches today. In our translation we have made that assumption and included the relevant doxology at the end of each psalm. Book V seems to have no brief doxology, so we anticipate using the Gloria Patri there.

Our Protestant English Bibles have 150 psalms in them, but there are in fact only 146 "whole psalms" in the psalter:

Psalms 9-10 are one psalm, an alphabetic acrostic moving through the Hebrew alphabet from the beginning of Psalm 9 to the end of Psalm 10.

Psalms 42-43 are clearly one psalm in three stanzas, as the refrain makes clear.

Psalms 32-33 are one psalm, for there is no title in Psalm 33, and they are linked in that Psalm32 says God will instruct, and then Psalm 33 provides the instruction in 22 lines—the number of letters in the Hebrew alphabet.

Psalms 70-71 are one psalm: Psalm 70 is virtually identical to Psalm 40:13-17, and this duplication makes sense only if it is the first part of Psalm 71, which again has no title.

Our Protestant arrangement follows the Hebrew text. Catholic and Orthodox Bibles follow the order of the Greek translation of the Hebrew text called the Septuagint, which combines and breaks up the psalms differently, resulting in different numbers for many of them. Comparing the Hebrew and the Septuagint shows us that in actual Temple practice, sometimes only part of a psalm might be sung. From the Bible we can also see that psalms were sometimes combined and rearranged, something we see in the composite psalms in 2 Samuel 22 and 1 Chronicles 16.

Looking at the 146 whole psalms, we find that the books of the psalter are significantly structured in their numerical totals:

> I: 17 + 22 (Hebrew alphabet)
> II: 17 + 12 (3 x 4)
> III: 17
> IV: 17
> V: 17 + 27 (3 x 3 x 3)
> or V: 22 + 22 (two x alphabet)

Seventeen is the sum of the two numbers of fullness, 7 and 10, and in I, II, and V another number related to fullness completes the count.

If we look at the order of the psalms, the same significant numbers turn up in Book V:

> Ps. 107-118 12
> Ps. 119 22 sections (alphabet)
> Ps. 120-136 17 (15 of ascent to Temple, and then two Temple praise)
> Ps. 137-150 14 (2 x 7)

All of this makes it clear that the final psalter has been very carefully structured, under divine inspiration.

Of the 146 whole psalms, the central two are 77 and 78. Psalm 77 ends with Moses and Aaron, and Psalm 78 ends with David. Each recounts history, first the history leading to the priestly covenant, and then the history leading to the kingly covenant. Both psalms focus on the exodus from Egypt, from an old world to a new. Psalm 77 ends in the wilderness. Psalm 78 ends at Mt. Zion, with David.

That this is the core of the psalter provides us a perspective on how the psalter begins. Psalm 1 is about priestly obedience, and Psalm 2 is about kingly reign. While these are two different psalms, they are designed to be read together on occasion, so that the righteous obedient man of Psalm 1 is, or becomes, the anointed king of Psalm 2.

Book 1 of the psalter consists of 17 + 22 psalms, while Book 5 consists of 22 + 22. There are 22 letters in the Hebrew alphabet and this is significant for Biblical theology and poetry. The second Person of God is the Word of God and also the Alphabet of God. As He says in Revelation, "I am Alpha and Omega, the beginning and the end" (see Revelation 1:8; 21:6; 22:13). These are the first and last letters in the Greek alphabet. In Hebrew, they are 'aleph and tav.

In the Ark of the Covenant in the Holy of Holies was the Word of God made stone. Corresponding to this Ark-chest was a box on the chest of the High Priest, the pouch of the Ephod. Inside the pouch were stones called 'Urim and Thummim, two words that begin respectively with 'aleph and tav. These two letters summarize the alphabet, which in turn is a symbol of the whole Word of God from beginning to end. Israel would consult God's Word either through the written Bible, or through the casting of the lots 'Urim and Thummim.

The psalter begins with Psalm 1. Psalm 1 begins with the word "Blessed" (*'ashre*) and ends with the word "perish" (*to'bher*). The first word begins with 'aleph, and the last word begins with tav.

Spun out from this are several alphabetic-acrostic psalms. Psalms 25, 34, and 145 begin each line with a successive letter of the alphabet, for a total of 22 lines. (So does Proverbs 31:10-31.) Psalm 9-10 is also an alphabetic-acrostic, though a few letters are missing. Psalm 37 and Lamentations 4 assigns two lines to each successive letter. In Lamentations 1 and 2, three lines are given to each letter. In Lamentations 3, three successive lines are given to each letter, and in Psalm 119 we find eight lines per letter. Finally, Psalms 33 and 38 (and Lamentations 5) have exactly 22 lines, though not alphabetically ordered. This seems no accident. Nahum 1 also includes a broken alphabetic-acrostic.

Since Psalm 1 introduces not only the psalter but also Book 1 of the psalter, it may be significant that all but two of the alphabetic psalms occur in Book 1, to wit: alphabetic- acrostic: Pss. 9-10, 25, and 34; non-acrostic: Pss. 33 and 38.

There are seven acrostic psalms in the psalter: Pss. 9-10, 25, 34, 111, 112, 119, and 145. Since Psalm 119 uses each letter eight times, the total with the other six single-use Psalms is fourteen (2x7) acrostic usages.

The Titles of the Psalms

We have translated and included the titles of each psalm, on the assumption that these are part of the God-given inspired text. We are aware that in some circles this is a disputed point, but we have chosen to err on the side of caution and tradition.

We have also, however, followed the research of James William Thirtle, in his book The Titles of the Psalm: Their Nature and Meaning Explained (Second Edition, New York: Henry

Frowde, 1905), as regards these titles. Thirtle made a good case, building on Habakkuk 3, that "Prayer of Habakkuk the prophet, according to Shigionoth" comes at the head of the psalm, and "For the Director, upon my stringed instruments" comes at the end. While Thirtle's book has often been overlooked, his thesis has met with some favor, and we have provisionally adopted it here.

Selah

While the meaning of the term "selah" continues to be disputed, we have found R. W. Landis's essay "The Meaning and Use of Selah" in The Danville Review (June, 1864), pp. 214-247, to be of the most help. He argues rather convincingly that the world "selah" indicates that the first lines of the psalm are to be repeated as a kind of refrain. We are very largely convinced, and have followed his advice here.

Some Translational Decisions

'Ashre. The first word in the psalter is usually translated "blessed," but this is confusing because barakh is also translated "blessed." 'Ashre also connotes "happy," and that is what some translations use. The same is true of the Greek makarios in the Beatitudes. We have decided to use the phrase "blest and merry."

It would be nice if we could find one English word that would do, but we have not found it thus far. We remember how Archbishop Thomas Cranmer, in translating the Latin prayers for the English Book of Common Prayer, often used two words for one Latin word. We have followed his principle.

Hesed. Here we have the word traditionally rendered "lovingkindness," which today is often argued to be better rendered "covenant faithfulness" or even something like "kinship commitment." We have stuck with the tradition, since many still argue for it, and it seems best to us.

Zamar. Usually translated something like "praise," this is the word from which "psalm" is derived. It sounds like the playing of an instrument, and the word "psalm" in both Hebrew (mizmor) and Greek (psallo) means something sung with an instrument. In fact, there is no evidence anywhere in the Bible that anything was sung to God without instruments. We have rendered zamar as "play music."

We have rendered 'elohim as "God," 'el as "Mighty One," 'adonai as "My Master," 'elyon as "Most High," and 'eloah as "Mighty Protector." The Tetragrammaton YHWH we have put as "Yahweh." We intend this for reading and singing the Psalms, not for Christian prayer, for the Name we have been given to use as a memorial name is Jesus, not Yahweh.

Notes on Chanting
Paul Buckley

Unlike most of the music that Westerners now sing and listen to—whether classical or pop, country or rock, jazz or old hymns—psalm chanting has no regular rhythm that you can tap your toes to. That doesn't mean it has no rhythm at all: Its rhythm is the *irregular* rhythm of the spoken word.

That can be confusing, even for people who read music, if they've never chanted a psalm. They may see a whole note on the page and think "four beats." But the notes in a psalm chant don't signify numbers of beats. Their time values are open-ended. Take a look at the tone for Psalm 1. The first note, like the first note of most tones here, is a whole note. It's where the first line of each couplet begins. In verse 1, that whole note lasts only as long as it takes to sing the words "Blest and merry"—four syllables (but not four beats). In verse 4, that same whole note lasts only as long as it takes to sing the word "Not"—a single syllable.

So if you read music, the first thing to remember is that in the world of psalm tones, *notes indicate pitch only, not time values.* They tell you what note to sing but not how long to sing it. The *text* is in the driver's seat, not a preset rhythmic pattern.

The way we wed psalm tone to psalm text—involving decisions about when to quit that first whole note and move on to the next notes and with which syllable to land on the last note—is called *pointing.* There's no one right way to point a psalm. But the aim is to keep the flow of the text as natural as possible from the first syllable to the last. And that means getting verbal accents and musical accents lined up. The English composer Henry Walford Davies put the goal this way: "read singingly: sing readingly."

If you're new to chanting, Psalm 2B is a good place to begin. It uses one of the simplest musical patterns, sometimes called Simplified Anglican Chant. Each line of the psalm is sung to only two notes. Here is the first line:

Why do the nations con- | spire

Every syllable before the vertical line is sung to the first note, which is often called the *reciting note.* The vertical line is the cue to sing what follows—the second syllable of *conspire* in this case—to the next note. That's typical: We sing most of the line on the first note and move to the second when we reach the last accented syllable. And then we're ready to go on to the next line of text and to the next couple of notes (a new reciting note and a new final accent).

Here are the first four lines of the psalm:

> Why do the nations con- | spire,
> And the peoples murmur a vain | thing?
> Positioned are the earth's | kings,
> And rulers take counsel to- | gether,

To put it in a way that highlights the musical pattern:

> First note (reciting note) | second note (final accent)
> Third note (reciting note) | fourth note (final accent)
> Fifth note (reciting note) | sixth note (final accent)
> Seventh note (reciting note) | eighth note (final accent)

A few things to note:

1. The accented syllable sung at the end of a line may be only a portion of a word (*-spire*), a one-syllable word (*thing, kings*), or an accented syllable trailed by one or more unaccented syllables (*-gether*). Sometimes—as in verses 4, 5, and 9—the last accented syllable launches a whole short phrase:

   > *scoffs at them*
   > *terrifies them*
   > *smash them*

2. The vertical line is no more than a signal to begin the next series of notes. It does not indicate a pause of any kind. Of course there are lines in the psalms where a pause at the vertical line makes sense for verbal reasons. Psalm 125:5 is an example:

   > Yahweh will lead them away with the troublemakers. | Peace • be upon • Israel.

   But the vertical line itself should never be approached as if it were a speed bump. Ordinarily, sing right through it to the next note.

3. The eight notes of the tone—four pairs—cover four psalm lines.

If Psalm 2B is among the simplest in this psalter, Psalm 2 introduces a scheme that is far more common. Each line uses four notes instead of only two. Here again are the first four lines:

> Why do | nations con-spire,
> > And peoples murmur a | VAIN thing?
> Positioned are | EARTH'S kings,
> > And rulers take | counsel to-gether,

Psalm 2 and Psalm 2B have this much in common:

1. What comes before a vertical line is sung to a whole note (the reciting note).
2. The vertical line tells us to move on from that note.
3. The last accented syllable of a line and the last note of the musical phrase coincide.

But 2 and 2B are pointed differently because of how the tone is structured, and there are a few new things to note:

1. This tone is bookended by the usual reciting note and final accent, but between them come two *transitional notes*. (Many transitional notes in this psalter appear as quarter notes, some as eighths, and a few as halves.) To highlight the new pattern:

> Reciting note | two transitional notes → final accent
> Second reciting note | two transitional notes → final accent

2. In the first line, *nations* is sung to the first transitional note, the first syllable of *con-spire* to the second, and the second syllable of *conspire* to the final note of the phrase. The hyphen in *con-spire* is the signal that the two syllables are sung to two notes. Compare the fourth line, which goes with the second half of the tone:

> And rulers take | counsel to-gether

Counsel is sung to the first transitional note. The first syllable of *to-gether* is sung to the second transitional note. And the last two syllables of *to-gether* go with the final note. Again, the hyphen cues us that *to-* and *-gether* are sung with two different notes.

3. In the second line, *vain* appears as VAIN. Those boldface uppercase letters indicate that a single word (or syllable) is sung to *both* transitional notes. Why? Because of colliding accents. The line here ends with *vain thing*, and both *vain* and *thing* are accented syllables. To ensure that *vain* gets the weight it needs and isn't treated musically as if it were unaccented, we spread it over two notes. Compare "EARTH'S kings" in the third line. (Note: In a few cases, a WORD is sung to more than two notes, as in Psalm 1:3, where DOES takes three notes.)

4. The eight notes of the tone—two sets of four—cover a couplet.

Bullets are another important typographical cue. Here is the third verse of Psalm 2:

> Saying, "Let us | break their chains,
> And throw | off of us ◆ Their ropes!"

We know what to do with the first line: Sing everything to the left of the vertical line to the reciting note, sing *break their* to the two transitional notes, and sing *chains* on the final note. Now for the second line: The bullet signals that the whole phrase *off of us* goes with the first transitional note. After that, we move on as usual: *Their* on the second transitional note, *ropes* on the final note. The first line needs no bullet: three words—*break their chains*—follow the vertical line and go neatly with the two transitional notes and final accent.

Sometimes an additional bullet further clarifies groupings, as in Psalm 47:5:

> Yahweh amidst the | sound ◆ of a ◆ trumpet.

The word *sound* goes with the first transitional note, *of a* with the second, and *trumpet* with the final note. This is the pattern:

> Reciting note | first transitional note ◆ second transitional note ◆ final accent

To summarize what is ordinarily the case, with a few additional notes:

- ◆ A vertical line | is the cue to move from a reciting note to a transitional note.
- ◆ **BOLD CAPS** indicate that a single syllable is sung to two or more notes.
- ◆ One or more hyphens within a word indicate that the separated syllables are sung to separate notes: *a-way* (two notes), *med-i-tates* (three notes).
- ◆ Similarly, words separated by a bullet ◆ are sung to separate notes.
- ◆ Many of the doxologies conclude in this way:

> A- | ◆ ◆ men!
> Yes! | A-men!

In the first line, we begin singing the first syllable of *Amen* on the reciting note. The two bullets that follow indicate that we keep singing that syllable on the two transitional notes before settling on the final accent with *-men*. In other words, the first syllable is sung to three notes. In the second line, notice that the **A**- is in boldface type: It's sung to both transitional notes.

- A cross (†) indicates that a verse is to be sung as a coda, using the second part of the chant as indicated in the score.
- An ellipsis … at the end of a page indicates that the psalm continues on the following page.

If all this sounds more complicated than it's worth, be assured that it is not. After singing psalms for a while, you'll begin to get a feel for it. Sooner or later, you may well find that you can pick up a psalm not included here and sing it with one of the tones, even without the benefit of vertical lines and bullets and so forth.

Nothing here is set in stone. You may want to experiment with different harmonies in the accompaniments, or you may think a line could be pointed better. Experiment away! But above all, sing the psalms.

BOOK I

Psalm 1

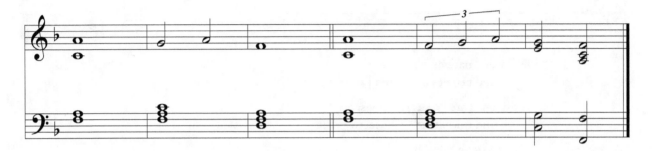

1   Blest and merry | is the | man,
         Who walks not in the counsel | OF the | wicked.

       And in the way of sinners | does not | stand,
         And in the seat of mockers | DOES not | SIT;

2   But rather in Yahweh's Instruction is | his de- | light,
         And on His Instruction he | med-i-tates | day and ◆ night.

3   And he is like a tree planted by | streams of | waters,
         Who yields his | fruit in his | season,

       And his leaf | does not | wither,
         And whatever he | DOES | prospers.

4   Not | so the | wicked!
         But rather they are like the chaff that | Spir-it–wind | blows a-way.

5   Therefore the wicked will not | stand in ◆ the | judgment,
         Nor sinners in the congregation | OF the | righteous.

6   For Yahweh knows the | way of ◆ the | righteous,
         But the way of the | wick-ed shall | perish.

       *Praise to Yahweh, the | God of | Israel.
         From everlasting and unto | E-ver- | lasting.

       A- | ◆ ◆ | men
         Yes! | A-- | MEN!

---

*Psalm chants have historically ended with a *Gloria Patri*. The closing doxologies in the Theopolis Psalter mostly come from the Psalter itself. Each Psalm in Book 1 (Psalms 1-41) ends with the closing words of this section of the Psalter, Psalm 41:13.

Psalm 2

1   Why do | nations con-spire,
     And peoples murmur a | **VAIN** thing?

2   Positioned are | **EARTH'S** kings,
     And rulers take | counsel to-gether,

   A- | **GAINST** Yahweh,
     And a- | gainst ♦ His a-nointed;

3   Saying, "Let us | break Their chains,
     And throw | off of us ♦ Their ropes!"

4   The One enthroned in the | heavens laughs;
     My | Mas-ter scoffs at them!

5   Then He | speaks to them ♦ in His ♦ wrath,
     And in His burning | anger He terrifies them.

6   Saying, "I Myself have in- | stalled My King,
     On Zion, My | ho-ly hill."

7   I will de- | clare the statute:
     Yahweh | said to Me,

   "My | Son You are,
     I Myself to- | day have ♦ be-gotten You.

8   Ask of Me and I will make | nations Your ♦ in-heritance,
     And Your possession the | ends of earth.

9   You will rule them with an | i-ron scepter.
     Like a vessel of | clay will ♦ You smash them."

10 Now therefore, O | kings, be wise;
     Be warned, you | judges of earth.

11 Serve | Yahweh with fear,
     And ex- | ult with trembling.

12 Kiss the Son, | lest He ♦ be angry,
     And you | perish in ♦ the way,

   For His wrath can flare | up in ♦ a moment.
     Blest and merry are all those who take | refuge in Him.

   Praise to Yahweh, the | God of Israel!
     From everlasting and | unto ever-lasting.
   A- | ♦ ♦ men!
     Yes! | A-men!

Psalm 2 B

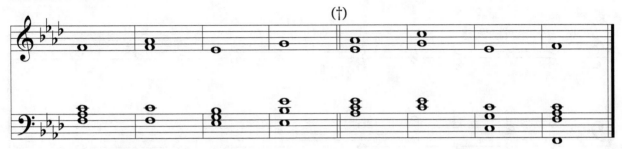

1   Why do the nations con- | spire,
        And the peoples murmur a vain | thing?

2   Positioned are the earth's | kings,
        And rulers take counsel to- | gether,

    Against | Yahweh,
        And against His a- | nointed;

3   Saying, "Let us break Their | chains,
        And throw off of us Their | ropes!"

4   The One enthroned in the heavens | laughs;
        My Master | scoffs at them!

5   Then He speaks to them in His | wrath,
        And in His burning anger He | terrifies them.

6   Saying, "I Myself have installed My | King,
        On Zion, My holy | hill."

7   I will declare the | statute:
        Yahweh said to | Me,

    "My Son You | are,
        I Myself today have be- | gotten You.

8   Ask of Me and I will make nations Your in- | heritance,
        And Your possessions the ends of | earth.

(†) 9   You will rule them with an iron | scepter.
        Like a vessel of clay You | smash them."

10 Now therefore, O kings be | wise;
        Be warned, you judges of | earth.

11 Serve Yahweh with | fear,
        And exult with | trembling.

12 Kiss the Son, lest He be | angry,
        And you perish in the | way,
    For His wrath can flare up in a | moment.
        Blest and merry are all those who take refuge in | Him.

    Praise to Yahweh, the God of | Israel!
        From everlasting and unto ever- | lasting.
    A- | men!
        Yes! A- | men!

Psalm 3

A psalm of David, as he fled from the face of Absalom, his son.

1   Yahweh, how many are my | foes!
       How many are rising | up a- | gainst me!

2   How many are saying of my | soul,
       "There is no salvation for | him in | God."

Selah   Yahweh, how many are my | foes!
       How many are rising | up a- | gainst me!

3   But it is You, Yahweh, who are a shield a- | round me,
       My Glory, and the One lifting | up my | head.

4   With loud voice to Yahweh I | cry,
       And He hears me from His | holy | mountain.

Selah   Yahweh, how many are my | foes!
       How many are rising | up a- | gainst me!

5   I myself lie down and | sleep;
       I awake because | Yahweh sus- | tains me.

6   I will not fear myriads of | people,
       Who on all sides are | set a- | gainst me.

7   Arise, | Yahweh!
       Deliver me, | O my | God!
    For You have struck all my enemies on the | jaw;
       The teeth of the un- | godly You have | broken.

(†) 8   From Yahweh is the de- | liverance!
       On Your people | is Your | blessing.

Blessed be Yahweh, the God of | Israel,
       From everlasting and | unto ever- | lasting;
A- | men!
       Yes! A- | men.

Psalm 4

A Psalm. By David.

1   When I call, answer me, my | right-eous God!
    From the distress | give me ⁙ re-lief.
        To me be merciful, and | hear my prayer.

2   You boys, how long will my | glory ⁙ be shamed?
    How long will you | **LOVE** worthlessness?
        How long will you | **SEEK** falsehood?

Selah   When I call, answer me, my | right-eous God!
    From the distress | give me ⁙ re-lief.
        To me be merciful, and | hear my prayer.

        Pause

3   Now know that Yahweh has separated the | godly to ⁙ Him-self;
        Yahweh will hear | when I call to Him.

4   Be angry, and | do not sin.
        Search within your heart when you are on your bed, | and be still.

Selah   When I call, answer me, my | right-eous God!
    From the distress | give me ⁙ re-lief.
        To me be merciful, and | hear my prayer.

        Pause

5   Sacrifice righteous com- | mun-ion meals,
        And | **TRUST** Yahweh.

6   Many are saying, "Who will | show us good?
        Let light from Your countenance | shine upon ⁙ us, Yahweh!"

7   You have put | gladness in ⁙ my heart,
        More than any season when their grain and | wine in-creased.

8   Peacefully composed I will lie | down and sleep,
        For it is You, Yahweh, alone who make me | dwell in safety.

    Praise to Yahweh, the | God of Israel!
        From everlasting and | unto ⁙ ever-lasting.
    A- | ⁙ men!
        Yes! | A-men!

Psalm 5

A Psalm. By David.

1   To my words give | **EAR**, Yahweh;
        Con- | sider my groaning.

2   Listen to the sound of my plea, my | King and ◆ my God,
        For to | You I pray.

3   Yahweh, it morning: You | hear my voice;
        It is morning: I lay my request be- | fore You ◆ and wait.

4   For You are not a Mighty One who takes | pleasure in wickedness.
        The wicked may not | dwell with You.

5   The arrogant will not stand be- | fore Your eyes.
        You hate all who | **MAKE** trouble.

6   You destroy those who | **SPEAK** falsehood.
        The man of blood and deceit Yah- | weh ab-hors.

7   But as for me, by Your abundant lovingkindness I will | enter Your house.
        I will bow toward Your holy temple in | fear of You.

8   Yahweh, lead me | in Your righteousness.
        On account of those who lie in wait for me, make straight Your | way be-fore me.

9   Because in his mouth is | no-thing trustworthy.
        their inward | part is ◆ des-truction.
    An open | grave is ◆ their throat.
        With their tongue they | speak de-ceit.

10   Hold them | guilty, O God!
        Let them fall by their | own in-trigues!
    For their multitudes of trans- | gres-sions, banish them,
        Because they are re- | bellious a-gainst You.

11   But let all who take refuge in | You be glad;
        Everlastingly let them | sing for joy.
    And spread Your pro- | tec-tion over them,
        That those who love Your Name may ex- | ult in You.

12   For it is You who bless the | righteous man, Yahweh.
        Like a shield, with | favor You ◆ sur-round him.

Praise to Yahweh, the | God of Israel!
    From everlasting and unto | ever-lasting.
A- | ◆ ◆ men!
    Yes! | A-men!

Psalm 6

A Psalm. By David.

1   Yahweh, do not re- | buke me in ◆ Your anger,
       Nor in Your | **WRATH** chasten me.

2   Be gracious to me, Yahweh, for I am | pining a-way
       Heal me, Yahweh, for my | bones are agonizing.

3   And my soul is in | **GREAT** anguish;
       But You, | Yahweh, how long?

4   Turn, Yahweh! | Rescue my soul!
       Save me because of Your | lov-ing-kindness!

5   For in death there is no me- | morial for You;
       In Sheol who will | give You thanks?

6   I am | weary with ◆ my sighing;
   All night long I | flood my bed;
       With my tears I | drench my couch.

7   Weak with sorrow | grows my eye;
       It is becoming old because of | all my adversaries.

8   Depart from me, all you who | **MAKE** trouble!
       For Yahweh has heard the | sound of ◆ my weeping.

9   Yahweh has heard my | sup-pli-cation;
       Yahweh ac- | cepts my prayer.

10   Disgraced and greatly dismayed are | all my enemies!
       They turn back, dis- | **GRACED** suddenly!

      Praise to Yahweh, the | God of Israel!
         From everlasting and | unto ever-lasting.
      A- | ◆ ◆ men!
         Yes! | **A**-men!

Psalm 6 B

Psalm
by David

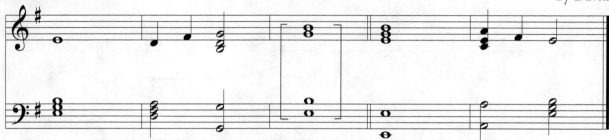

1 Yahweh, do not re- | buke me in ⋅ Your anger,
   Nor in Your | **WRATH** chasten me.

2 Be gracious to me, Yahweh, for I am | pining a-way;
   Heal me, Yahweh, for my | bones are agonizing.

3 And my soul is in | **GREAT** anguish;
   But You, | Yahweh, how long?

4 Turn, Yahweh! | Rescue my soul!
   Save me because of Your | lov-ing-kindness!

5 For in death there is no Me- | morial for You;
   In Sheol who will | give You thanks?

6 I am | weary with ⋅ my sighing;
   [All night long I flood my bed;]
       With my tears I | drench my couch.

7 Weak with sorrow | grows mine eye;
   It becomes old because of | all my adversaries.

8 Depart from me, all you who | **MAKE** trouble!
   For Yahweh has heard the | sound of ⋅ my weeping.

9 Yahweh has heard my | sup-pli-cation;
   Yahweh ac- | cepts my prayer.

10 Disgraced and greatly dismayed are | all my enemies!
   They turn back, dis- | **GRACED** suddenly!

   Praise to Yahweh, the | God of Israel!
   From everlasting and | unto ever-lasting.
   A- | ⋅ ⋅ men!
       Yes! | **A**-men!

Psalm 12

Psalm
by David

1   Help, Yahweh, for the godly person | is no more;
        For the faithful disappear from among the | sons of Adam.

2   Emptiness they speak to | one an-other.
        Flattering lips: With double | heart they speak.

3   May Yahweh cut off all | flatter-ing lips,
        The tongue that speaks | GREAT things;

4   That say, "With our tongue we | will pre-vail;
        "We own our lips— | who is ◆ our master?"

5   "Because of the op- | pression of ◆ the weak,
        "Because of the | groaning of ◆ the needy,

    "I will a- | rise," says Yahweh;
        "I will protect him from the | one who ma-ligns him."

6   Yahweh's sayings are | PURE sayings;
        Silver purified in an earthen furnace, refined | sev-en-fold.

7   You, | Yahweh, will ◆ guard them;
        You will preserve us from this gener- | ation ever-lastingly.

8   On every side the wicked | strut a-bout,
        When vileness is exalted among the | sons of Adam.

    Praise to Yahweh, the | God of Israel!
        From everlasting and | unto ever-lasting.
    A- | ◆ ◆ men!
        Yes! | A-men!

For the Director.

Psalm 19

Psalm
by David

1 The heavens are declaring the | Mighty One's glory;
And the work of His hands is pro- | claimed by ♦ the firmament.

2 Day after day it | pours forth speech,
And night after night it dis- | **PLAYS** knowledge.

3 There is no speech and | there are ♦ no words;
Un- | heard is ♦ their sound.

4 Into all the | earth goes ♦ their line,
And to the end of the | world their utterances.

For the sun He has placed a | tent in them,
5 And he is like a bridegroom coming | forth from his ♦ pa-vilion;

He rejoices like a mighty man to | run his course.
6 At the end of the | heavens is ♦ his rising,

And his circuit is to their | oth-er end;
And there is nothing | hid from ♦ his heat.

Pause

7 Yahweh's In- | struction is perfect,
Re- | storing the soul.

Yahweh's | testimonies are certain,
Making | wise the simple.

8 Yahweh's | precepts are right,
Re- | joicing the heart.

Yahweh's com- | mandments are radiant,
En- | lightening the eyes.

9 The fear of | Yahweh is clean,
En- | during for-ever.

Yahweh's | laws are true,
Alto- | geth-er righteous.

10   They are more | precious than gold,
  And more than | much fine gold;

And | sweeter than honey,
  Even drippings from | ho-ney-combs.

11   Moreover, Your servant is il- | lumined by them;
  In guarding them is | great re-ward.

Pause

12   Errors | who can ⁕ dis-cern?
  From | hidden ones ⁕ for-give me!

13   Also from presumptuous acts keep | back your servant;
  Let them not | RULE over me.

Then | I shall ⁕ be blameless,
  And I shall be innocent of | great trans-gression,

14   May they be pleasing—the words of my mouth and the meditation of my heart—
be- | fore You, Yahweh,
  My | Rock and ⁕ my Kinsman.

Praise to Yahweh, the | God of Israel!
  From everlasting and | unto ever-lasting.
A- | ⁕ ⁕ men!
  Yes! | A-men!

For the Director.

Psalm 23

Psalm
by David

1   Yahweh | is my Shepherd,
        Nothing | shall I lack.

2   In green pastures He | makes me ⁺ lie down;
        Beside quiet | waters He leads me.

3   My soul | He re-stores;
        He leads me in righteous | paths for ⁺ His Name's sake.

4   Even though I walk in a valley of deep darkness, I will | fear no evil;
        For | You are with me,

    Your rod and Your | staff, they comfort me.
5   You prepare before me a table in the | presence of ⁺ mine enemies.
    You fatten my | head with oil;
        My | cup o-verflows.

6   Only goodness and mercy will follow me all the | days of ⁺ my life,
        And I shall dwell in Yahweh's house to the | end of days.

    Praise to Yahweh, the | God of Israel!
        From everlasting and | unto ever-lasting.
    A- | ⁺ ⁺ men!
        Yes! | A-men!

Psalm 25

by David

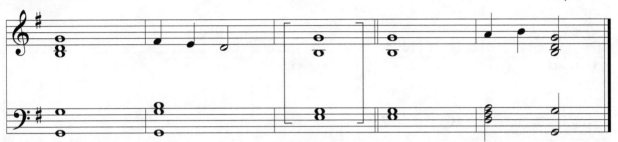

'aleph

1 To You, | **Yah**-weh!
   I lift up my | soul, my God.

beth

2 In You I trust, do not | let me ⋆ be shamed;
   Do not let my enemies | tri-umph over me

gimel

3 Indeed none of those who wait for | You will ⋆ be shamed;
   Those will be shamed who deal treacherously with- | **out** cause.

daleth

4 Your ways, | Yah-weh, show me!
   Your | **paths**, teach me!

he

5 Lead me in Your | faithfulness ⋆ and ⋆ teach me,
   [For You are the God of my salvation;]
      You are the one I a- | wait ⋆ all the day.

zayin

6 Remember Your mercies, Yahweh, and Your | lov-ing-kindnesses,
   For they are | ever-lasting.

heth

7 Sins of my youth and my transgressions do | not re-member;
   [According to Your loving-kindness remember me,]
      Because of Your | good-ness, Yahweh.

teth

8 Good and | upright is Yahweh;
   Therefore He instructs | sinners in ⋆ the way.

yodh

9 He leads the af- | flicted in justice,
   And He teaches the af- | flicted His way.

kaph

10 All the paths of Yahweh are loving- | kindness and faithfulness,
    For those who guard His | covenant and ⋆ His testimonies.

lamedh

11 For Your | Name's sake, Yahweh,
    Pardon my liability, for | it is great.

Psalm 25 (cont.)

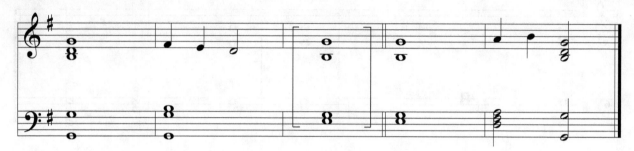

mem

12 Who is the man who | FEARS Yahweh?
   He will instruct him in the | way he ◆ should choose.

nun

13 His soul will a- | bide in ◆ the good,
   And his seed will in- | herit the land.

samekh

14 The secret counsel of Yahweh is for | those who fear Him,
   And His covenant He | MAKES known to them.

'ayin

15 My eyes are always | turned to Yahweh,
   For He will bring my feet | out of ◆ the net.

pe

16 Turn to me and be | gracious to me,
   For lonely and af- | flicted am I.

tsaddeh

17 The troubles of my | heart are ◆ en-larged;
   From my dis- | tress-es free me!

resh

18 Look upon my af- | fliction and ◆ my toil,
   And for- | give all ◆ my sins.

19 Look at my enemies, how | they have ◆ in-creased!
   And they hate me with | vio-lent hatred.

shin

20 Guard my | soul and ◆ de-liver me;
   Do not let me be shamed, for I take | refuge in you.

tav

21 Let integrity and uprightness preserve me, for I | wait for You.
22   Redeem Israel, O God, out of | all his troubles.

Praise to Yahweh, the | God of Israel!
   From everlasting and | unto ever-lasting.
A- | ◆◆ men!
   Yes! | A-men!

Psalm 36

by the Servant of Yahweh
by David
An Oracle

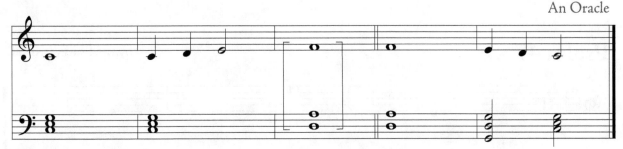

1   The transgression of the wicked person is my | med-i-tation:
    There is no fear of God be- | fore his eyes.

2   For he flatters himself in his | **OWN** eyes,
    Hating to de- | tect his ⁺ lia-bility.

3   The words of his mouth are | trouble and ⁺ de-ceitful.
    He has ceased to be wise, to | **DO** good.

4   Trouble he | plots on ⁺ his bed.
    [He commits himself to a course not good;]
    Evil he does | not re-ject.

5   Yahweh, in the heavens is Your | lov-ing-kindness,
    Your faithfulness is up to the | **HIGH** clouds.

6   Your righteousness is like the | might-y mountains;
    [Your justice like the great deep.]
    Both mankind and cattle You pre- | **SERVE**, Yahweh.

7   How priceless is Your loving- | kindness, O God!
    Yes, the sons of Adam in the shadow of Your | wings find refuge.

8   They feast on the a- | bundance of ⁺ Your house,
    And the river of Your delights You | give them ⁺ to drink,

9   For with You is the | fountain of life.
    In Your light | we see light.

10 Continue Your lovingkindness to | those who know You,
    And Your righteousness to the | upright in heart.

11 May the foot of the proud not | come a-gainst me.
    And let not the hand of wicked persons | drive me ⁺ a-way.

12 Behold how they lie | fallen, the troublemakers!
    Thrown down, un- | able to rise!

    Praise to Yahweh, the | God of Israel!
    From everlasting and | unto ever-lasting.
    A- | ⁺ ⁺ men!
    Yes! | A-men!

Book II

For the Director
by the Sons of Korah
Psalm

Psalm 47

1 All peoples, | CLAP hands!
  Shout to God with the | voice of triumph!

2 For Yahweh, Most | High, is awesome;
  A great King over | all the earth.

3 He subdues | peo-ples under us,
  And populations | under our feet.

4 He chooses our in- | heritance for us,
  The excellence of Jacob, | whom He loves.

Selah All peoples, | CLAP hands!
  Shout to God with the | voice of triumph!

5 God has ascended a- | midst a shout,
  Yahweh amidst the | sound ⬩ of a ⬩ trumpet.

6 Play | music to God!
  Play | MU-sic!

7 Play | music ⬩ to our ⬩ King!
  Play | MU-sic!

8 For the King of all the | earth is God!
  Play music for a | DEEP truth.

9 God | reigns over nations;
  God sits on His | ho-ly throne.

10 The princes of the peoples have | gathered to-gether
  As the people of the | God of Abraham.
For the shields of the earth be- | long to God.
  He has as- | cended to ⬩ the highest.

*Blessed be Yahweh, the | God of Israel,
  Who alone does | WON-ders.
And blessed be His glorious | Name ever-lastingly,
  And filled with His glory be | all the earth.
A- | ⬩ ⬩ men!
  Yes! | A-men!

---

*Psalm chants have historically ended with a *Gloria Patri*. The closing doxologies in the Theopolis Psalter mostly come from the Psalter itself. Each Psalm in Book 2 (Psalms 42-72) ends with the closing words of this section of the Psalter, Psalm 72:18-19.

Psalm 50

A Psalm. By Asaph.

1   The Mighty One, | **GOD**, | Yah-weh speaks,
        And He | sum-mons | THE | EARTH,
     From the rising of the | sun to ◆ its | setting.

2   Out of Zion, the per- | fection of | beauty, | God shines ◆ forth.

3   Our God comes and will | not keep | silent.
     A fire de- | vours be- | fore Him,
        And all a- | round Him ◆ it | STORMS | mighti-ly.

4   He summons the | heavens | above,
        And the earth, that | He may | judge His | people:

5   "Gather to | **ME** | My saints,
        Those cutting My covenant | by Com- | munion | Sacri-fice."

6   And the heavens de- | clare His | right-eousness,
     For | God Him- | self is | **JUDGE**.

Selah   The Mighty One, | **GOD**, | Yah-weh speaks,
        And He | sum-mons | THE | EARTH,

7   "Hear, My people, | and | I ◆ shall speak;
     O Israel, and I shall | testify a- | bout you.
        I My- | self am | **GOD**, | your God.

8   Not for your Communion Sacrifices do | I re- | buke you,
        Or for your Ascensions, | which are ◆ be- | fore Me ◆ con- | tinual-ly.

9   I will not | take from ◆ your | house ◆ a bull,
        From your | FOLDS | any | GOATS.

10   For Mine is | every | for-est beast,
     The | cattle | of a | thousand hills.

11   I know | every | moun-tain fowl,
        And the | FIELD | insect is | MINE.

12   If I were hungry, | I would ◆ not | tell you;
        For | Mine is ◆ the | world and | all in ◆ it.

13   Do I | eat the | flesh ◆ of bulls,
        And the | blood of | GOATS | do I ◆ drink?

14   Sacrifice to | God a | Thanks-giving,
        And perform to the Most | High your | Votive | Offer-ings.

15   And call upon Me in the | day of | trouble;
        I will deliver you, and | you will | glo-ri- | fy Me."

◆ ◆ ◆

Psalm 50 (cont.)

16 But to the | wick-ed | says God:
    "What right have you to de- | clare My | stat-utes,
        Or to | take My | cove-nant | on your ◆ lip?

17 For you | hate in- | struc-tion,
        And | cast My | words be- | hind you.

18 When you see a | thief, you | join ◆ with him.
        With a- | dulter-ers | is your | LOT.

19 Your mouth you send | out in | evil,
        And your tongue you | harness | to de- | CEIT.

20 You take the chair and | speak against ◆ your | brother;
        To your own mother's | son you | give out | slander.

21 These things you did, and | I kept | si-lent;
    You thought the | I AM ◆ was | like you.
        I will rebuke you and ac- | cuse you ◆ be- | fore your | EYES.

22 Now consider this, you who forget the | Mighty Pro- | tector
        Lest I tear you in pieces, and | there be | none to ◆ de- | liver;

23 Whoever sacrifices Thanksgivings | glo-ri- | fies Me;
        And the one preparing a way, I will show | him the ◆ sal- | vation of | GOD."

Praise to Yahweh, the | God of | Is-rael,
    Who a- | LONE | WORKS | wonders.
And praise to His glorious | Name ever- | last-ingly.
    And let His | glory | FILL | all the ◆ earth.
A- | ◆ ◆ | MEN!
    Yes! | A- | ◆ ◆ | MEN!

Psalm 56

By David. Miktim. When Philistines seized him in Gath.

1   Be gracious, O God, for mere man pants | af-ter me;
  All day long, fighting he op- | pres-ses me.
2   My foes pant | all day long.
  Indeed, many are fighting a- | gainst me ⬧ from the ⬧ heights.
3   In the day that | I am ⬧ a-fraid,
  I am one who puts my | trust in You,
4   In God—I | praise His Word!
  In God I | put my trust.
 I shall not | be a-fraid.
  What can | flesh ⬧ do to ⬧ me?
5   All day long my | words they twist;
  Against me all their | thoughts are ⬧ for evil.
6   They | stir them-selves ⬧ up;
  They | lurk in secret.
 They are the ones who | watch my heels,
  When they lie in | wait for ⬧ my life.
7   Through such troublemaking should they | be de-livered?
  In anger put down the | peoples, O God!
8   Of my wanderings You Yourself have | **KEPT** count.
  Put my tears in Your bottle; are they not | in Your book?
9   Then my enemies will turn back in the | day when ⬧ I call;
  This I know, because | God is for me.
10   With God I | praise The Word.
  With Yahweh I | praise The Word.
11   In God I trust; I | do not fear.
  What can mankind | do to me?
12   Upon me, O God, | are Your vows:
  I shall render a | Thanksgiving to You.
13   For You have delivered my | soul from death,
  Have you not kept my | feet from stumbling?
 So that I can walk before the | face of God
  In the | light of life.

 Praise to Yahweh God, the | God of Israel,
  Who alone | **WORKS** wonders.
 And praise to His glorious | Name ever-lastingly.
  And let His glory fill | all ⬧ the earth.
 A- | ⬧ ⬧ men!
  Yes! | **A**-men.

Psalm 65

1   For You, even silence is praise, O | God in Zion;
2   [And to You will be performed a vow, O You who hear prayer.]
        To You | all flesh comes!
3   Deeds causing liability pre- | vail a-gainst me.
        Our transgressions | You have covered.
4   Blest and merry is the one You | choose and ◆ bring near;
        He | dwells in ◆ Your courts.
    We are filled with the | good things of ◆ Your house,
        With the | holiness of ◆ Your temple.

5   By awesome deeds in | righteousness ◆ You ◆ answer us,
        O God of | our sal-vation—
    The trust of all the | ends ◆ of the ◆ earth,
        And of the | farthest seas—
6   Establishing | mountains ◆ by His ◆ power;
        Arming Him- | self with strength;
7   Stilling the | roaring of ◆ the seas,
        [The roaring of their waves,]
            Even the | tumult of ◆ the peoples.
8   They are in awe who dwell at the ends, be- | cause of ◆ Your wonders.
        The outgoings of the morning and the evening You make | shout for joy.

9   You | visit the earth,
        And cause it to | o-ver-flow;
    Greatly | You en-rich it—
        God's river is | full of water.
    You pre- | pare their grain.
        In this way | You pre-pare it:
10   Its furrows You | water a-bundantly;
        Its | ridges You level;
    With | showers You soften it;
        Its growth | **You** bless.

◆ ◆ ◆

Psalm 65 (cont.)

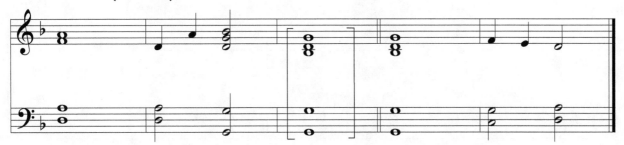

11   You crown the | year with ⬩ Your goodness,
        And Your cart paths | drop with fatness.

12   Dripping are the | grasslands ⬩ of the ⬩ desert,
        And with joy the hills | clothe them-selves.

13   Covered are the | meadows with flocks,
        And the valleys | deck themselves ⬩ with grain.
    They | shout for | joy;
        Yes, | **THEY** | sing!

Blessed be Yahweh, the | God of Israel,
    Who alone does | **WON**-ders.
And blessed be His glorious | Name ever-lastingly,
    And filled with His glory be | all the earth.
A- | ⬩ ⬩ men!
    Yes! | A-men!

For the Director.

Psalm 66

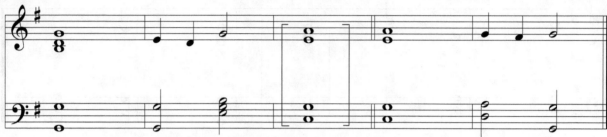

1   Sing joyfully to God, | all the earth!
       Play music to the | glory of ⬦ His Name!
    Set forth glory: | **His** praise!

2   Say to God: How | fearful are ⬦ Your works!
    So great is Your power that Your enemies | cringe be-fore You.
       All the earth | bow themselves ⬦ be-fore You;

3   And play | musics to You;
       They play | musics to ⬦ Your Name.

Selah   Sing joyfully to God, | all the earth!
       Play music to the | glory of ⬦ His Name!

    Pause

4   Come and see the | works of God,
       Fearful dealings among the | sons of Adam.

5   He turned the sea into | **dry** land;
       Through the river they | passed on foot;
    There | we re-joiced in Him!

6   He is ruling by His | might ever-lastingly;
    His eyes on the | nations keep watch.
       Let not the re- | bellious ex-alt themselves!

Selah   Sing joyfully to God, | all the earth!
       Play music to the | glory of ⬦ His Name!

    Pause

7   Bless our | God, O peoples,
       Make the sound of His | praise be heard,

8   He is setting our lives a- | mong the living,
       And has not let our | **feet** slip.

9   For You have | tried us, ⬦ O God;
       You have refined us as | silver is ⬦ re-fined.

10   You brought us | into the net;
       You laid an oppressive burden up- | on our hips.

⬥ ⬥ ⬥

Psalm 66 (cont.)

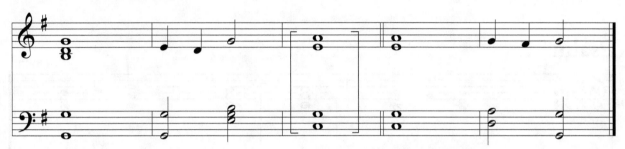

11 You caused a mere man to | ride at ◆ our heads!
    We went through | fire and ◆ through water,

12 And You brought us out | into a-bundance.

13   I will come to Your | house with ◆ As-censions;

14 I will pay You my vows, which my | **LIPS** uttered,
    And My mouth spoke when | I was in ◆ dis-tress.

15 Ascensions of fatlings will I send up to You with the | smoke of rams;
    I will provide cattle with | **MALE** goats.

Selah Sing joyfully to God, | all the earth!
    Play music to the | glory of ◆ His Name!

  Pause

16 Come, hear, and I will tell all who | **FEAR** God
    What He has | done for ◆ my soul.

17 To Him I | cried with ◆ my mouth
    And lifted | up with ◆ my tongue.

18 If I had cherished troublemaking | in my heart,
    My | Master would ◆ not have ◆ heard;

19 But certainly | God has heard;
    He has given heed to the | sound of ◆ my prayer.

20 Blessed be God, who has turned away | neither my prayer,
    Nor His loving- | kindness from me.

Blessed be Yahweh, the | God of Israel,
    Who alone does | **WON-** | ders.
And blessed be His glorious | Name ever-lastingly,
    And filled with His glory be | all the earth.
A- | ◆ ◆ men!
    Yes! | **A**-men!

For the Director.
With stringed instruments.

Book III

Psalm 77

by Asaph
Psalm

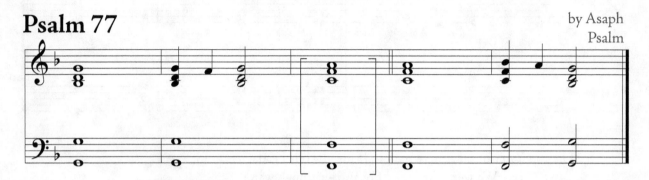

1   My voice: to God, and I | cry a-loud.
    My voice: to | God, and + He + hears me.

2   In my day of distress, I | seek my Master.
    [My hand at night is stretched out,]
        And without wearying my soul re- | fuses to + be comforted.

3   I memorialize | God and + I groan;
    I meditate and my | spirit grows faint.

Selah   My voice: to God, and I | cry a-loud.
    My voice: to | God, and + He + hears me.

4   You hold | open my eyelids.
    I am troubled and | cannot speak.

5   I con- | sider days + of old,
    Years | long a-go.

6   I memorialize by my stringed | instrument in + the night.
    [In my heart I meditate,]
        And my | spirit in-quires:

7   "Forever will my Master re- | ject?
    And never show | favor a-gain?

8   Has His lovingkindness | ceased per-petually?
    Has His promise failed to be for generation after | gener-ation?

9   Has the Mighty One for- | gotten to + be merciful?
    Has He withheld His | compassions in anger?"

Selah   My voice: to God, and I | cry a-loud.
    My voice: to | God, and + He + hears me.

10   And I said, "My ap- | peal is this:
    The years of the Most | High's right hand."

11   I will memorialize the | deeds of Yah.
    Yes, I will memorialize Your wonders of | long a-go,

✦ ✦ ✦

Psalm 77 (cont.)

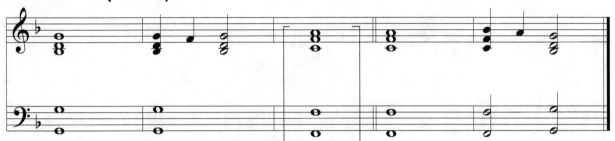

12   And I will meditate on | all Your work.
      And Your mighty | deeds I will ✦ con-sider:

13   O God, in | holiness is ✦ Your way.
      Who is a mighty one as | great as God?

14   You are the Mighty One who per- | FORMS wonders.
      You display among the | peoples Your power.

15   You redeemed with Your | arm Your people,
      Sons of | Jacob and Joseph.

Selah   My voice: to God, and I | cry a-loud.
      My voice: to | God, and ✦ He ✦ hears me.

16   Waters | saw You, God.
      Waters | saw You. ✦ They writhed.

      Indeed, | depths were ✦ con-vulsed.
17   Clouds | poured down waters.

      Sound the | skies gave forth.
      Indeed, Your arrows | flashed a-round.

18   Sound of Your | thunder: ✦ in the ✦ whirlwind.
      [Lightnings lit up the world.]
      The earth | trembled and quaked.

19   Through the | sea was ✦ Your path,
      [And Your ways through mighty waters.]
      And Your footprints were | NOT | seen.

20   You led Your | people ✦ like a ✦ flock,
      By the hand of | Moses and Aaron.

      *Praised be Yahweh ever- | lastingly! A- | men!
      Yes! | A-men!

*Psalm chants have historically ended with a *Gloria Patri*. The closing doxologies in the Theopolis Psalter mostly come from the Psalter itself. Each Psalm in Book 3 (Psalms 73-89) ends with the closing words of this section of the Psalter, Psalm 89:52.

Psalm 79

Psalm
by Asaph

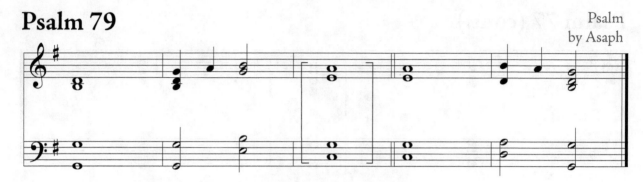

1   O God, nations have | come into ⁘ Your in-heritance,
        [They defiled Your holy Temple.]
            They made Je- | rusalem into ruins.

2   They gave the bodies of Your servants as food for the | fowls of ⁘ the heavens,
        The flesh of Your devoted ones for the | beasts of ⁘ the earth.

3   They poured out their blood like water all a- | round Je-rusalem,
        And there was no one to per- | FORM burial.

4   We have become objects of | taunting to ⁘ our neighbors,
        Mockery and derision to | those a-round us.

5   How long, Yahweh? Will You be | angry per-petually?
        Will Your jealousy | burn like fire?

6   Pour out Your wrath on the nations that | do not ⁘ ac-knowledge You,
        On kingdoms who do not | call on ⁘ Your Name.

7   For he de- | VOURED Jacob,
        And his | homeland they devastated,

8   Do not remember against us the lia- | bilities of ⁘ our fathers.
        [Speedily let Your compassion come to meet us,]
            For we are | brought very low.

9   Help us, | God of our ⁘ sal-vation!
        [For the reputation of the glory of Your Name, even deliver us,]
            And pardon our | sins for ⁘ Your Name's ⁘ sake.

10   Lest the nations say, | "Where is ⁘ their God?",
        [Before our eyes make known among the nations]
            The vindication of Your servants' | out-poured blood.

11   Let the groans of the prisoners | come be-fore You.
        By the greatness of Your arm preserve the | sons of death.

12   Return sevenfold into the | bosoms of ⁘ our neighbors
        The taunts with which they taunted | You, my Master.

13   Then | we, Your people,
        Even the | sheep of ⁘ Your pasture,
   Will give You | thanks for-ever.
        Generation after generation we will re- | count Your praise.

    Praised be Yahweh ever- | lastingly! A-men!
        Yes! | A-men!

BOOK IV

Psalm 98

1   Sing to Yahweh a | **NEW** song,
     For He has done | wonder-ful things,
        His Salvation–worker is His right hand and His | ho-ly arm.

2   Yahweh has made | known His ✦ Sal-vation;
        Before the eyes of the nations He has re- | vealed His righteousness.

3   He has remembered His lovingkindness and His faithfulness to the | house of Israel;
        All the ends of the land have seen the Sal- | vation of ✦ our God.

4   Shout joyfully to Yahweh, | all the land;
        Break forth and sing for joy and | **PLAY** music.

5   Play music to Yahweh | with the lyre;
        With the lyre and the | voice of song.

6   With trumpets and the | sound of ✦ the ✦ ram's horn
        Shout joyfully before the | **KING**, Yah-weh

7   Let the sea roar | and its fullness,
        The world and | those ✦ who ✦ dwell in her.

8   The rivers: let them | clap their hands;
        The mountains all together: let them sing for | joy be-fore Yahweh.

9   For He is coming to | judge the land.
     He will judge the | world with righteousness,
        And the | peoples with equity.

     *Praise to Yahweh, the | God of Israel,
        From everlasting and | unto ever-lasting.
     And let all the people | say A-men.
        Praise Yah, | Halle-lu-Yah!

---

*Psalm chants have historically ended with a *Gloria Patri*. The closing doxologies in the Theopolis Psalter mostly come from the Psalter itself. Each Psalm in Book 4 (Psalms 90-106) ends with the closing words of this section of the Psalter, Psalm 106:48.

Psalm 100

Psalm. By David.

1   Make a joyful noise to | Yahweh, ◆ all the | land!

2   Serve | **YAH-** | weh with | gladness;
Come be- | fore Him ◆ with | singing.

3   Acknowledge that | Yahweh, | He is | God.
It is He who | made us and ◆ we are | His;
His | people ◆ and the | sheep of ◆ His | pasture.

4   Enter His | gates with ◆ thanks- | giving;
His | **COURTS** | **WITH** | praise.
Give | thanks to | Him;
— | **BLESS** | **HIS** | Name.

5   For good is Yahweh; ever- | lasting is His ◆ loving- | kindness;
And generation after gener- | ation is | **HIS** | faithfulness.

Praise to Yahweh, the | God of | Israel,
From ever- | lasting and | unto ever- | lasting.
And let all the people | say A- | men.
Praise | Yah, Hal- | le-lu- | Yah!

BOOK V

Psalm 115

1 Not to us, Yahweh, not to | us,
    but to Your Name | give glory;
  Because of Your | love;
    Because of | Your truth.

2 Why should the nations | say,
    "Where, now, is | their God?"

3 Now, our God is in the | heavens;
    All that He pleases, | He does.

4 Their idols are silver and | gold,
    The work of | man's hands.

5 They have mouths, but they cannot | speak.
    They have eyes but they can- | not see.

6 They have ears, but they can- | not hear.
    They have noses by they can- | not smell

7 Their hands: they cannot | feel.
  Their feet: they cannot | walk.
    They cannot make a sound with | their throat.

8 Those who make them are | like them,
    Everyone who | trusts in them.

Rhythmic section:

9 Israel, trust in | Yahweh!
    Their help and their shield | is He.

10 House of Aaron, trust in | Yahweh!
    Their help and their shield | is He.

11 Fearers of Yahweh, trust in | Yahweh!
    Their help and their shield | is He.

12 Yahweh remembers | us;
  He | will bless.
  He will bless the house of | Israel.
    He will bless the house | of Aaron.

✦ ✦ ✦

Psalm 115 (cont.)

Rhythmic section continued:

13   He will bless the fearers of | Yahweh,
         The small together with | the great.

14   May Yahweh make you in- | crease,
         You and | your children.

15   May you be blessed by | Yahweh,
         Maker of heaven | and earth.

Non-rhythmic:

16   The heavens are Yahweh's | heavens,
         But the earth He has given to the sons | of man.

17   The dead do not | praise Yah,
         Nor do any who go down | into silence.

18   But as for us, we will | bless Yah
         From this time forth and ev- | er-lastingly.

*Glory to the Father, and to the | Son,
         And to the Ho- | ly Spirit,
As it was in the beginning, is now, and ever | shall be,
         Age after age. | A-men.

*Each Psalm in Book 5 ends with the traditional Trinitarian doxology, the *Gloria Patri.*

Psalm 120

A Song of the Ascents

1   To Yahweh in my dis- | tress I cried,
    And He | **HEARD** me.
2   Yahweh, deliver my soul from | lying lips,
    From a de- | ceit-ful tongue.

3   What will He | do to you,
    What will He add further to you, you | **FALSE** tongue?
4   Sharp arrows of the | mighty man,
    With firebrands of the | **BROOM** tree!

5   Woe is me, that I | sojourn in ⋅ Meshech,
    I dwell among the | tents of ⋅ Ke-dar!
6   Too long has my soul dwelt with one who | **HATES** peace.
7   I am for peace; but when I speak, | they are ⋅ for ⋅ war.

Glory to the Father, | and to ⋅ the ⋅ Son,
    And to the | Ho-ly Spirit,
As it was in the beginning, is | now, and ⋅ ever ⋅ shall be,
    Age after | age. A-men.

Psalm 121

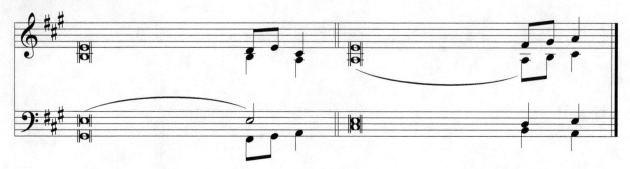

1. Shall I lift up mine | eyes to ⬩ the mountains.
    Whence | comes my help?
2. My | help is ⬩ from Yahweh,
    Who shaped | heaven and earth.

3. He will not allow your | foot to ⬩ be moved,
    He will not | slumber ⬩ who ⬩ guards you.
4. Behold, | He will ⬩ not slumber,
    And He will not sleep, | Guardian of Israel.

5. Yahweh | is your Guardian.
    Yahweh is your Shade at your | RIGHT hand.
6. By day the | sun will ⬩ not ⬩ strike you,
    Nor the | moon by night.
7. Yahweh will guard you from | ALL evil:
    He will | guard your soul.
8. Yahweh will guard your | go-ing out,
    And your | com-ing in.
    From | this time forth,
    And | ev-er-lastingly.

Glory to the Father, | and to ⬩ the Son,
    And to the | Ho-ly Spirit,
As it was in the beginning, is | now, and ⬩ ever ⬩ shall be,
    Age after | age. A-men.

Psalm 121B

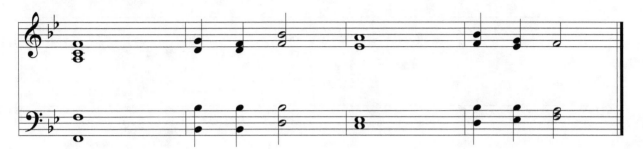

A Song for the Ascents

1   Shall I lift up mine | eyes to ⬩ the mountains.
        Whence | comes my help?
2   My | help is ⬩ from Yahweh,
        Who shaped | heaven and earth.

3   He will not allow your | foot to ⬩ be moved,
        He will not | slumber ⬩ who ⬩ guards you.
4   Behold, | He will ⬩ not slumber,
        And He will not sleep, | Guardian of Israel.

5   Yahweh | is your Guardian.
        Yahweh is your Shade at your | RIGHT hand.
6   By day the | sun will ⬩ not ⬩ strike you,
        Nor the | moon by night.
7   Yahweh will guard you from | ALL evil:
        He will | guard your soul.
8   Yahweh will guard your | go-ing out,
        And your | com-ing in.
    From | this time forth,
        And | ev-er-lastingly.

Glory to the Father, | and to ⬩ the Son,
        And to the | Ho-ly Spirit,
As it was in the beginning, is | now, and ⬩ ever ⬩ shall be,
        Age after | age. A-men.

Psalm 122

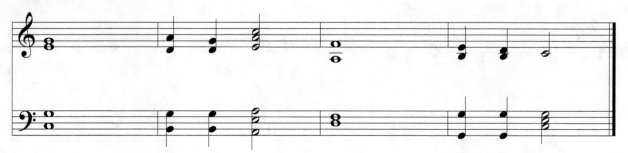

A Song of the Ascents, of David.

1 I rejoiced with those who said to me, "To Yahweh's house | let us go!"
2 Our feet are standing in your | gates, Je-rusalem.

3 Jerusalem is being | built • like a • city:
   She is com- | pacted to-gether.
4 There as- | cend the tribes—
   The | tribes of | Yah!
   To the | Testimony of Israel,
   To give thanks to | Yah-weh's Name.
5 For there are set up | thrones for judgment,
   Thrones of the | house of David.

6 Pray for the | peace of • Je-rusalem:
   "May they | prosper • who • love you.
7 "Peace be with- | in your walls,
   "Prosperity with- | in your citadels."
8 For the sake of my brethren and companions, I now say: | "Peace be • with-in you."
9 For the sake of the house of Yahweh our God, I will | seek your good.

Glory to the Father, | and to • the Son,
   And to the | Ho-ly Spirit,
As it was in the beginning, is | now, and • ever • shall be,
   Age after | age. A-men.

Psalm 123

A Song of the Ascents

1   Unto You I | lift up ✦ mine eyes,
        Who | dwell in ✦ the ✦ heavens.

2   Behold, as the eyes of servants to the | hand of ✦ their masters,
        As the eyes of a maid to the | hand of ✦ her mistress,
    So our eyes are to | Yahweh our God,
        Until He shows | mercy to us.

3   Have | mercy on ✦ us, Yahweh!
        Have | mercy on us!
    For we are exceedingly | filled ✦ with con-tempt;

4   Our soul is ex- | ceeding-ly filled,
    With the scorn of | those who ✦ are at ✦ ease,
        With the con- | tempt of ✦ the proud.

Glory to the Father, | and to ✦ the Son,
    And to the | Ho-ly Spirit,
As it was in the beginning, is | now, and ✦ ever ✦ shall be,
    Age after | age. A-men.

Psalm 124

1   If it had not been Yahweh who was for us—Let Israel now | say:

2   If it had not been Yahweh who was for us when men rose up a- | gainst us,

3   Then they would have swallowed us a- | live,
    When their wrath was kindled a- | gainst us.

4   Then the waters would have over- | whelmed us;
    The torrent would have swept over our | soul.

5   Then it would have gone over our | soul—
    The raging | waters!

6   Praise | Yahweh!
    Who has not given us as prey to their | teeth.

7   Our soul has escaped like a | bird,
    From the snare of the | fowlers.

    The snare is | broken,
    And we have es- | caped.

8   Our help was in Yahweh's | Name,
    Who made heaven and | earth.

    Glory to the Father, and to the | Son,
    And to the Holy | Spirit,
    As it was in the beginning, is now, and ever | shall be,
    Age after age. A- | men.

Psalm 124B

A Song of the Ascents, of David.

1 If it had not been Yahweh who was for us—Let | Israel now say:

2 If it had not been Yahweh who was for us when | men rose ⋅ up a-gainst us,

3 Then they would have | swallowed ⋅ us a-live,
   When their | wrath was ⋅ kindled a-gainst us.

5 Then the waters would have | o-ver-whelmed us;
   The torrent would have | swept ⋅ over our ⋅ soul.

7 Then it would have gone | over our soul—
   The | rag-ing waters!

9 Praise | **Yah**-weh!
   Who has not given us as | prey ⋅ to their ⋅ teeth.

7 Our soul has es- | caped ⋅ like a ⋅ bird,
   From the | snare ⋅ of the ⋅ fowlers.
   The | snare is broken,
   And | we have ⋅ es-caped.

8 Our help was in | Yah-weh's Name,
   Who | made ⋅ heaven and ⋅ earth.

   Glory to the Father, | and to ⋅ the Son,
   And to the | Ho-ly Spirit,
   As it was in the beginning, is | now, and ⋅ ever ⋅ shall be,
   Age after | age. A-men.

Psalm 125

A Song of the Ascents.

1   Those who trust in Yahweh are | like Mount Zion,
        Which cannot be moved, but ever- | lastingly a-bides.

2   As the mountains sur- | round Je-rusalem,
        So Yahweh sur- | rounds His people,
    From | this time forth,
        And | ev-er-lastingly.

3   For the scepter of wickedness will not rest on the land al- | lotted ◆ to the ◆ righteous,
        Lest the righteous reach out their | hands to ◆ in-justice.

4   Do good, Yahweh, to | those ◆ who are ◆ good,
        Even to those who are | upright in ◆ their hearts.

5   As for such as turn aside to their | crook-ed ways,
        Yahweh will lead them away with the troublemakers. | Peace ◆ be upon ◆ Israel.

Glory to the Father, | and to ◆ the Son,
    And to the | Ho-ly Spirit,
As it was in the beginning, is | now, and ◆ ever ◆ shall be,
    Age after | age. A-men.

Psalm 126

A Song of the Ascents.

1 When Yahweh brought back the cap- | tivity of Zion,
  We were like those re- | stored to health.

2 Then our mouth was | filled with laughter,
  And our tongue with a | joy-ful song.
 Then they said a- | mong the nations,
  "Great things | Yahweh ✦ has ✦ done for them."

3 Great things | Yahweh has ✦ done for ✦ us;
  We were | MER-ry.

4 Turn, Yahweh, | our cap-tivity,
  Like the | streams in ✦ the south.

5 Those | sowing in tears,
  With a joyful | song will reap.

6 Going forth, he goes forth weeping, bearing | seed for sowing;
  Returning, he returns with a joyful song, | bearing his sheaves.

Glory to the Father, | and to ✦ the Son,
 And to the | Ho-ly Spirit,
As it was in the beginning, is | now, and ✦ ever ✦ shall be,
 Age after | age. A-men.

Psalm 127

A Song of the Ascents, of Solomon.

1   Unless | Yahweh ◆ builds a ◆ house,
        In vain they | labor ◆ who ◆ build it.
    Unless | Yahweh ◆ guards a ◆ city,
        In vain the watchman | stays a-wake.

2   It is vain for you being | early to rise,
        Being late to | STAY up,
    Eating the | bread of sorrows,
        For He gives His be- | lov-ed sleep.

3   Behold, a heritage from | Yahweh are children;
        A reward is the | fruit of ◆ the womb.

4   Like arrows in the | hand ◆ of a ◆ warrior,
        So are the children of | ONE'S | youth.

5   Blest and merry is the man whose | quiver ◆ is ◆ full of them.
        They will not be shamed when they speak with | adversaries ◆ in the ◆ gate.

    Glory to the Father, | and to ◆ the Son,
        And to the | Ho-ly Spirit,
    As it was in the beginning, is | now, and ◆ ever ◆ shall be,
        Age after | age. A-men.

Psalm 128

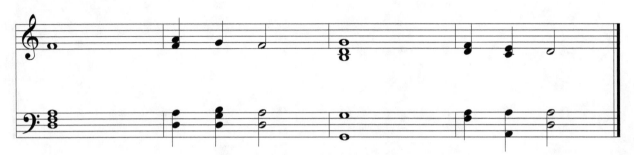

A Song of the Ascents.

1 Blessed is every one who | **FEARS** Yahweh,
  Who | walks ✦ in His ✦ ways.

2 Of the labor of your palms you | will in-deed eat,
  Merry blessings and | good things ✦ will be ✦ yours.

3 Your wife: like a fruitful vine in- | side your house.
  Your children: like olive plants a- | round your table.

4 Behold, that | **THUS** blest
  Is the strong-man who | **FEARS** Yahweh.

5 Yahweh | bless you ✦ from Zion.
  And may you see the good of Jerusalem all the | days of ✦ your life.

6 And may you see your | chil-dren's children.
  Peace | be up-on ✦ Israel!

Glory to the Father, | and to ✦ the Son,
  And to the | Ho-ly Spirit,
As it was in the beginning, is | now, and ✦ ever ✦ shall be,
  Age after | age. A-men.

Psalm 129

A Song of the Ascents.

1 Many a time have they afflicted me from my youth—Let | Israel now say:
2   Many a time have they afflicted me from my youth,
        yet they have not pre- | vailed a-gainst me.
3 On my back the | plow-ers plowed;
        They | lengthened their furrows.

4 Yahweh is | **RIGHT**-eous;
        He has cut in pieces the | cords of ✦ the wicked.

5 May all be put to shame and turned back who | **HATE** Zion,
6   May they be like grass on housetops, which before it | **GROWS**, withers;
7 Which does not fill his | palm the reaper,
        Nor his | arms ✦ the ✦ sheaf-binder.
8 And may those who pass by not say, "The blessing of | Yahweh ✦ be up-on you;
        We bless you in the | Name of Yahweh"!

Glory to the Father, | and to ✦ the Son,
        And to the | Ho-ly Spirit,
As it was in the beginning, is | now, and ✦ ever ✦ shall be,
        Age after | age. A-men.

Psalm 130

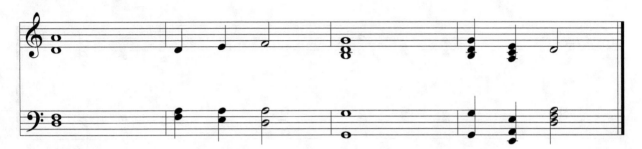

A Song of the Ascents.

1 From the depths I cry to You, Yahweh! | Master, • hear my • voice!
2   Let Your ears be attentive to the | sound of my • cries for • mercy.
3 If You recorded liabilities, Yah… | Master! • Who could • stand?
4   But with you is forgiveness, | so that • You are • feared.

5 I | wait for Yahweh;
      My soul waits, and | in His • Word I • hope.
6 My soul waits for the Master more than | watchmen • for the • morning;
      More than | watchmen • for the • morning.

7 Place your hope, O | Israel, in Yahweh,
      For with | Yahweh is • loving-kindness;
   And with Him is a- | bundant re-demption;
8   And He is the One who will redeem Israel from | all his • lia-bilities.

   Glory to the Father, | and to • the Son,
      And to the | Ho-ly Spirit,
   As it was in the beginning, is | now, and • ever • shall be,
      Age after | age. A-men.

Psalm 131

A Song of the Ascents.
By David.

1   Yahweh, not | proud is ◆ my heart,
        Not | haughty ◆ are mine ◆ eyes,
    And I do not go into | GREAT matters
        Or into things too pro- | found for me.

2   Surely | I have calmed,
        And | quieted my soul.
    Like a weaned child up- | on his mother,
        Like the weaned child up- | on me is ◆ my soul.

3   Put your hope, O | Israel, in Yahweh,
        From this time | forth and ◆ ever-lastingly.

Glory to the Father, | and to ◆ the Son,
    And to the | Ho-ly Spirit,
As it was in the beginning, is | now, and ◆ ever ◆ shall be,
    Age after | age. A-men.

Psalm 132

A Song of the Ascents.

1   Remember, Yahweh, for | David's sake,
     All his | pains-taking effort:
2   How he swore an | oath to Yahweh,
     And vowed to the | Valiant One ♦ of Jacob:
3   "Surely I will not go into the | chamber of ♦ my house;
     Surely I will not go up to the | comfort of ♦ my bed;
4   "Surely I will not give | sleep to ♦ mine eyes,
     To my | eye-lids slumber,
5   "Until I | find a ♦ place for ♦ Yahweh,
     Tabernacles for the | Valiant One ♦ of Jacob."

6   Behold, we | heard of ♦ it in ♦ Ephrathah,
     We found it in the | fields of Ja'ar.
7   Let us | go into ♦ His tabernacles;
     Let us worship at the | footstool ♦ of His ♦ feet.
8   Arise, | Yahweh, ♦ to Your ♦ resting place,
     You and Your | power-ful ark.
9   Let Your | priests be ♦ clothed with ♦ righteousness,
     And let Your | saints ♦ sing for ♦ joy.

10 For Your servant | David's sake,
     Do not turn away the | face of ♦ Your a-nointed.
11 Yahweh swore an oath to | David in truth,
     He will not | turn from it:
  "From the | fruits of ♦ your body,
     I will | place up-on your ♦ throne.
12 "If your sons will | guard My covenant
     And My testimony, which | I ♦ shall ♦ teach them,
  "Then their | sons for-ever
     Will sit up- | on your throne."

♦ ♦ ♦

Psalm 132 (cont.)

13 For | Yahweh has ◆ chosen Zion,
    He desired her for His | hab-i-tation:

14 "This is My | resting place ◆ for-ever,
    Here will I dwell, for | I have ◆ de-sired her.

15 "Her provision: | blessing ◆ I will ◆ bless,
    Her poor will I | satisfy with bread.

16 "Her priests will I | clothe with ◆ sal-vation,
    And her saints: singing for joy they will | sing for joy.

17 "Here will I make the | horn of ◆ David grow,
    I will prepare a | lamp for ◆ Mine a-nointed.

18 "His enemies will I | clothe with shame,
    But upon him will his | crown ◆ be re-splendent."

Glory to the Father, | and to ◆ the Son,
    And to the | Ho-ly Spirit,
As it was in the beginning, is | now, and ◆ ever ◆ shall be,
    Age after | age. A-men.

Psalm 133

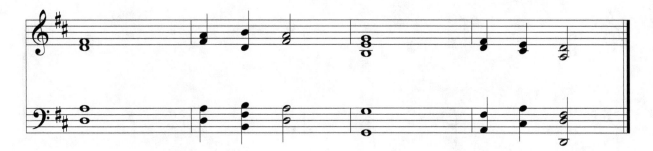

A Song of the Ascents.
By David.

1   Behold, how | good and ⋆ how pleasant,
        For brethren to dwell to- | gether in unity!
2   It is like the precious | oil up-on the ⋆ head,
        Descending | onto the beard,
    The | beard of Aaron,
        Descending onto the | edge of ⋆ his garments.
3   It is like the | dew of Hermon,
        Descending onto the | mountains of Zion;
    For there Yahweh com- | manded the blessing:
        Life | ev-er-lasting!

    Glory to the Father, | and to ⋆ the Son,
        And to the | Ho-ly Spirit,
    As it was in the beginning, is | now, and ⋆ ever ⋆ shall be,
        Age after | age. A-men.

Psalm 134

A Song of the Ascents.

1   Behold, praise Yahweh, all | servants of Yahweh,
        Who stand in Yahweh's | house at night!

2   Lift up your | hands ✦ at the ✦ sanctuary,
        And | PRAISE Yahweh.

3   Yahweh | bless you ✦ from Zion,
        Who made | heaven and earth.

Glory to the Father, | and to ✦ the Son,
    And to the | Ho-ly Spirit,
As it was in the beginning, is | now, and ✦ ever ✦ shall be,
    Age after | age. A-men.

Psalm 138

by David

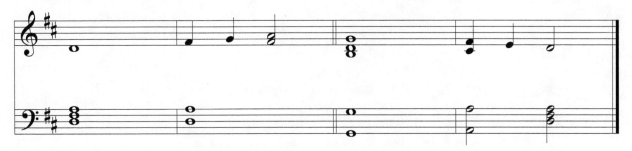

1 I will praise You with my | **WHOLE** heart;
   Before the gods I will sing | praises to You.

2 I will bow down toward Your | ho-ly temple,
   And | praise Your Name,

 For Your loving- | kindness ✦ and Your ✦ truth,
   Because You have magnified Your | Word above ✦ all Your ✦ Name.

3 In the day when I cried | out, You answered me,
   And made me bold with | strength ✦ in my ✦ soul.

4 All the kings of the | earth will ✦ praise You, ✦ Yahweh,
   When they hear the | words ✦ of Your ✦ mouth.

5 Yes, they shall | sing of the ✦ ways of ✦ Yahweh,
   For | great is ✦ Yahweh's ✦ glory.

6 Though Yahweh is on high, yet He re- | gards the lowly,
   But the | proud He ✦ knows from a-far.

7 Though I walk in the | midst of trouble,
   You will re- | **VIVE** | me.

 You will stretch | out Your hand,
   Against the | wrath ✦ of my ✦ enemies,

 And Your right | hand will save me.
8   Yahweh will per- | fect ✦ that which con-cerns me.

 Yahweh, Your loving- | kindness is ✦ ever-lasting;
   Do not forsake the | works ✦ of Your ✦ hands.

 Glory to the Father, | and ✦ to the ✦ Son,
   And to the | Ho-ly Spirit,
 As it was in the beginning, is | now, and ✦ ever ✦ shall be,
   Age after | age. A-men.

Printed in the USA
CPSIA information can be obtained
at www.ICGtesting.com
LVHW081918281023
762449LV00013B/1358